Printed
For
Quixote Press
by
BRENNAN PRINTING
100 Main Street
Deep River, Iowa 52222
515-595-2000

MISSISSIPPI RIVER PO' FOLK

By

Pat Wallace

QUIXOTE PRESS
R.R. #4
Box 33B
Blvd. Station
Sioux City, Iowa 51109

QUIXOTE PRESS
Bruce Carlson, Publisher
R.R. #4, Box 33B
Blvd. Station
Sioux City, Iowa 51109

PRINTED
IN
U.S.A.

Dedicated

to my

Mother Leona (Pope) Tourney

Little "Lonie-Girl", as Mom was nicknamed, grew up in the thirties in a midwestern river-town. Her childhood as one of the Mississippi's Po' Folk, though filled with hardship, was rich and exciting. Momma's family relied on a strong faith in God, honest sweat and toil . . . and grudgingly accepted occasional help from the local Relief Office to survive.

As a child, Momma enjoyed a freedom children of today do not know. Few of her playmates were entertained with toys. Most, like Momma, relied on their own imaginations and makeshift playthings.

They were a hardy lot, those Po' Folk. Perhaps the hardships they endured contributed to their strength of character, unshakable faith, and deep appreciation of life.

Pat Wallace

Table of Contents

The reader must appreciate the fact that these stories have never been published before. Some of them could cause embarrassment to living people today. Because of that, the stories use fictitious names. It should be understood that any similarity between those names and actual people, living or dead, is purely coincidental.

FOREWORD

This book is about a young girl's recollections of life along the Missouri and Illinois section of the Mississippi River is a collage of people and incidents out of the 1930s as seen through the eyes of a child.

These child-like visions of those hard times, recorded now, by that little girl's grown-up daughter, offers us new insights of those times and those places.

It's a book you better not start unless you have time to finish it. You'll find it hard to put down.

Professor Phil Hey
Briar Cliff College
Sioux City, Iowa

PREFACE

No, don't bother scratching your head to try to figure out who Leona Pope is. She isn't a famous lady of society of the arts. Her name isn't cast in a fancy bronze plaque on the cornerstone of any of our universities. She is simply a gracious lady living today in Hannibal, Missouri, who remembers what life was for a child growing up on the Grand Old Mississippi back in the '30s.

She recalls a slice of America back when children were pretty much left alone by the adults, when they were free to roam about as far as their skinny little legs would carry them, so long as they'd be back for bedtime. Leona's story is one that reminds us of the days when the hot summer sun warmed countless swimmin' holes for bronzed and carefree children.

The lives of Leona and her friends were but part of a bigger and crueler world their parents were painfully aware of. Poverty had a place at every table and in every bed. That hot summer sun was the same one that made ovens out of every shack; ovens for which there were no fans, or electricity to turn them.

America's giant bread basket proved an empty promise for fathers who saw one temporary job after another evaporate with a minutes notice and for mothers who used greens and water to stretch a few 'taters to cover another meal. To the children of the '30s, however, reality was "snitching" a watermelon from a poorly guarded patch, or a hand-me-down pair of shoes they could show off at school. That was the real world to the children of the '30s. That is the world Leona Pope shares with us in MISSISSIPPI RIVER PO' FOLK.

INTRODUCTION

Though I didn't realize it at the time, growing up in the thirties made me more fortunate than children of today. Even though the product of an already too-crowded household, I was lucky to have my large family for support and comfort. We were miserably poor. Moreover, we were poor AND living in the heart of the economically depressed Midwest.

I was a happy-go-lucky child; free to roam the perimeters of my hometown to my heart's content — as long as I made it back home by bedtime. Penniless, I would journey out on a long, lazy summer day and forage for myself. I could "snitch" a quick lunch from an unsuspecting grocer, or a tempting garden might woo me with its fresh watermelons.

Material possessions didn't matter much. What I valued most was the chance to explore the hills and hollers of my hometown . . . avidly reading a well-worn book, sampling a crisp Jonathan apple from a neighbor's orchard, venturing with shivering limbs through the cobweb ridden corridors of the local haunted house, and discovering that life can be as full and rich as one makes it.

Along the way, I made many friends and encountered numerous fascinating characters. This book is for them, and I hope its readers can appreciate the vivid recollections of the little girl named "Lonie".

Leona Pope Tourney

CHAPTER I

GRANDMAW AND POPPA SCHECKHORST

ntil the autumn of my eighth year, I had only a brief acquaintanceship with my maternal grandparents. Their farm, just south of Frankford, seemed a universe away to us, for it took half a day to get there from our house. Although our visits were infrequent, Grandmaw wrote weekly letters to Momma and her other children.

When Daddy came down with malaria that year, we were destitute. His job on the railroad would not await his recovery, and Momma tried desperately to keep us clothed and fed by herself. She

took in wash, cleaned at the fancy houses on the hill, and even tried to get a job at the button factory. Her meager earnings were never enough, and we soon realized we couldn't make it without help.

That's when Grandmaw and Poppa sent word that they wanted us to move in with them for a time. They weren't in much better shape than we, but still insisted we go to live on the farm with them.

Their farmhouse was a tiny four-room place, which was already crowded with Aunt Tillie's two boys. In those days, there was an unwritten law about taking care of one's family, and Grandmaw's worst fear was that we would end up in the county poorhouse over in Palmyra ... a fate, to her, much worse than death.

Grandmaw was an imposing figure. She towered over my grandfather, whom everything one affectionately called "Poppa". It was plain who wore the pants in their family, for Grandma had a will of iron and a backbone to match.

We knew, though, that tough as she was, that didn't mean we were safe from having the disgrace of having to go to the poor-house if things didn't get any better.

One of Poppa's favorite stories was about the time he first met Grandmaw. They were enroute to America from their native Germany, both having been indentured by Americans in need of cheap laborers. Grandmaw was slated to work at a boarding-house near Monroe City, Missouri; and Poppa had been consigned to a ranch in South Dakota somewhere.

At first, he took little interest in the tall, scrawny blonde girl who flirted with him. But after a time, Grandmaw managed to claim his attention in a unique manner. She approached him one day on the deck and complained that she had been pestered all through the journey by an unwanted suitor.

She told Poppa she had grown tired of the young man's constant pursuit and asked that he help her. Poppa agreed to escort her on board ship, so as to discourage the other young gentleman, and Grandmaw promised to pay him handsomely for the service. The notion of being paid for such "easy" work seemed ridiculous to Poppa, but he agreed.

In the course of their journey to America, Poppa grew to love Grandmaw. They were married on board ship, and Grandmaw confessed later that it was not Poppa she had hired to woo her, but the "pesky" suitor he thought he was discouraging. Throughout their married life, Poppa continued to tease her about his "pay" for the work he did.

After their arrival in the United States, Poppa

managed to get out of the contract for his work in South Dakota. Instead, he traveled to Missouri with Grandmaw.

Things were very difficult for them at first. Poppa could not find work, and they lived in a tent in a makeshift "village" with other foreigners not far from where the riverboat dropped them off.

When, at last, Grandmaw had worked off her passage, they moved to the farm near Frankford as tenant-farmers.

All of their wordly possessions were carried in a small washtub between them and they made the journey to their new home on foot. Their hard work and ambition paid off, and in a few years they had managed to save enough money to buy their own farm. Throughout their lives, the fact that that washtub grew to actually owning a bit of America was their greatest source of pride.

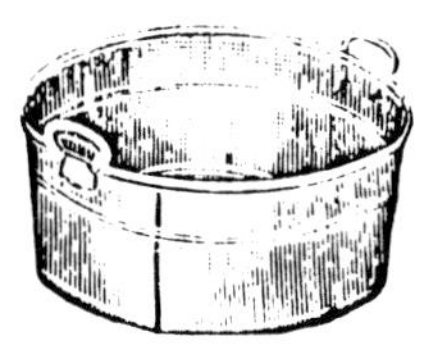

They both had very thick German accents, but I
quickly became accustomed to them. Grandmaw
and Poppa shared a closeness and bond that was
amazing. They seemed to read each other's
thoughts, and oftentimes, Grandmaw would fill
Poppa's glass or fetch his food without prompting.
They always drank from the same china coffee-
mug; one which had been carefully carried from
Germany. They vowed never to sip from the cup
again, should one of them die. Poppa was the one
who had to keep that vow.

Grandmaw was a devout Mennonite. She wore the
plain and long dresses that were common among

women of her faith.
She was even called
to preach on occa-
sion. In a sterm voice
with the distinct ac-
cent, she would com-
mand our whole
family to kneel in
prayer. I recall how
white her wood floor was from all the lye-water
scrubbings she had given it.

Daddy's malaria grew worse, and we began to
despair of a recovery. We had lived with Grandmaw and Poppa only a few months when it
became apparent that we would all starve to death
without extra money. That's when Grandmaw took
a job as a cook in a small restaurant in Frankford.
She would rise long before dawn each day and
make the long journey into town on root; returning long after sunset, totally exhausted. Momma

was put in charge of the household, and she worked furiously to please Grandmaw.

Grandmaw alway saw fit to re-do Momma's chores to suit her, often boxing Momma's ears in the process.

Poppa never seemed to work very hard. Aunt Tillie's two boys handled most of the farmwork, and Poppa gave them a free hand in running the place. Even my sisters and I were set to work, and I remember how it took two of us to work the plow-team. The huge walking plow

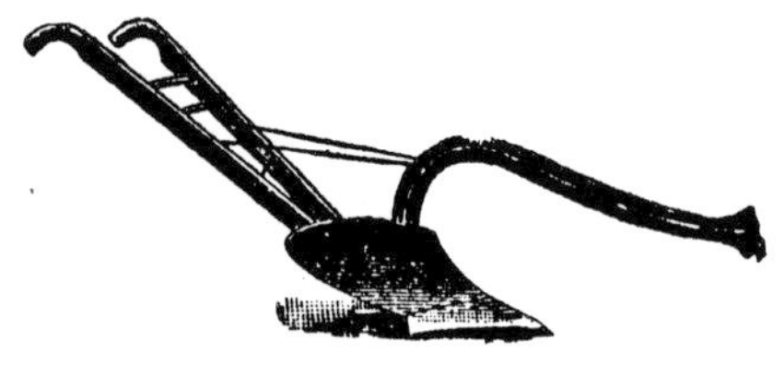

seemed to tower over us, and we would return from the fields and practically fall into bed each night.

Grandmaw's job provided just enough money to see us through that winter. When spring came, however, the restaurant closed down. She return- ed from work one night, in tears, and Poppa rac- ed from the house to console her.

"Now we be goin' to da poor-house, for sure! "I heard her wail.

We had boiled turnips and taters as our regular meal every day after that. There was no meat, even for seasoning, but the starchy vegetables were plentiful and filling. After each meal, Grand- maw would command us all to kneel and pray with her again, except that now she prayed more fervently than ever. Her prayer was "Make not my burdens lighter, but my shoulders broader". And she often cried as she prayed.

We were in dire straits, for even our supply of taters and turnips would eventually diminish. Still Grandmaw had an unshakable faith in the Lord.

After we had finished praying one evening, she rose happily. She told us God would provide as he saw fit and that she was going to bed without a care. Her burdens had been removed she said.

I wondered if she wasn't a bit too trusting at the time, and wondered, too, if God had been able to understand her prayer with the thick German accent.

The next day seemed an eternity. There was no breakfast for us when we rose, for God hadn't seen fit to provide it yet.

We set out to the fields with growling tummies and sad faces, while Grandmaw spent the morning trusting and praying. For our noon meal, Momma had managed to find some fresh greens, and the unseasoned mixture tasted as good as anything I'd ever eaten. We knelt and prayed with Grandmaw once more before returning to the fields and listened as she repeated her entreaties to God.

We seemed to spend an interminable amount of time on that floor but were finally allowed to rise, rubbing our knees to relieve the pain. I overhead Momma telling Grandmaw that there would be no more food that day. Grandmaw boxed her ears again and admonished her for not having faith.

We were filling our canteen from the well, when we spotted the cloud of dust from the road. That

meant company was on its way, for we could see
the dust from a vehicle long before it reached our
lane. Grandmaw timed her walk to the front gate
so as to arrive there just before our visitors did.

Several dusty old cars meandered single file down
the lane, and I recognized some of the people in
them as grandma's fellow Mennonites. They carried baskets and some crates to our front porch,
and there was so much food in those parcels, my
mouth began to water.

They had even brought a good supply of quinine
for Daddy's malaria.

Grandmaw began to dance then, even though her
religion prohibited it.

"See, didn't I tell you that God would provide us food today?"

Grandmaw's meaningful and glaring looks at Momma made Momma kind of get to studying the ground pretty hard.

After Grandmaw got done praising God for her good fortune, she hugged and kissed our benefactors one by one. Then she knelt in the yard again  and prayed with a voice choked with emotion. She made a point to tell God how unfaithful her family had been in his redemption, and how the baskets of food proved that He knew of their plan all along, in spite of their unfaithfulness.

That was the first miracle I had ever seen. For a long time afterward, though, I wondered why it had taken the Lord a whole day to get it done.

CHAPTER II

THE END OF THE WORLD

y Aunt Polly and Uncle Mick lived on the south end of Hannibal, on one of the tallest hills in our very little town. I guess progress took its own sweet time reaching them, because they had no running water, no electricity, nor any of the other "modern" conveniences. The hill their house sat on was so steep and winding that Daddy's old horse would always

balk right at the bottom of it. We would have to
tie the wagon up and climb the hill on foot.

As poor as we were then, Aunt Polly and Uncle
Mick were even poorer. Momma always packed
crates of food along for them, even though we

could ill afford it. Aunt Polly had seven youngins
and three grandchildren living at home. Without
Momma's generosity, I believe they would surely
have starved.

Just over the hill from their ramshackle house was
an old cemetery called "The Riverside". We used
to spend hours playing hide-and-seek there, dar-
ting behind the huge headstones. The major attraction of the place was running water. Near the
center of the cemetery, a hydrant protruded. This
was where Aunt Polly got all of their water, and
they had to haul it home in buckets.

The one chore that I along with my
cousins was required to do at Aunt
Polly's was to go after water with
that bucket. It was a back-breaking
job, for that huge wooden bucket
was already heavy. When filled with

water, we found it darned near impossible to drag back to the house. Then, too, there was the problem of having to enter that cemetery after dark when the place became quite spooky.

Other than the going-after-water chore, I was always delighted to spend time at Aunt Polly's. The occasion for my doing that was that now and then, Aunt Polly would send some of her children to stay with Momma and Daddy, and some of us would go to Aunt Polly's. If it wasn't for that practice, Aunt Polly's children would never have ventured beyond their hilltop home.

I don't recall that Uncle Mick ever had a real job. He sort of hung around home a lot and got in Aunt Polly's way. Now and then, he would be called upon to go over to the cemetery and make ready a grave. Course, his two oldest boys did most of the hard diggin' while Mick supervised. One part of the cemetery was especially rocky and tough to dig, so Uncle Mick tried to keep a grve open and ready there all the time. That way, he could stay one step ahead of business, and perhaps avoid being called upon to prepare a grave at a moment's notice. As soon as the grave had been occupied, he would dispatch his boys to prepare another. There was always an open, ready grave somewhere in the cemtery.

Every night before bedtime, we were sent to fetch water home. It didn't help matters any that my sister, Pearl, would recall — out loud — every ghost story she'd ever heard while enroute to the hydrant. We always managed to make the journey back a bit faster, and never cared much that our buckets had sloshed half their contents out on the way.

Pearl was a steady churchgoer in those days. It's not that she had a heap of religion or anything, but just that Momma felt she, in particular, needed redeeming. Pearl had been somewhat troublesome during her childhood, and then, at least, on Sunday mornings, Momma knew she was well occupied and out of trouble.

Pearl memorized the Scripture verses required and told me how her Sunday School class had been studying the verses about the end of the world. She feared that day might overtake us unawares, and constantly spoke about it.

One late summer evening, as we carried our bucket over to the cemetery, I guess those Scriptures were pretty fresh in Pearl's mind. We reached the hydrant, and, as usual, were pumping our buckets full, when the strangest sound we'd ever heard drifted in to us. I could see Pearl's eyes glowing in the dark, wide with fear, and she didn't even blink. She began to pump that hydrant furiously, overflowing the bucket in the process.

"Probably an old hoot owl", she remarked, trying to be brave for me, I'm sure.

The sound came again . . . it was a low, moaning noise, and definitely not the sound an owl makes.

Pearl had a brave image to maintain for me; I suppose that's what prompted her to investigate the noise.

We started off across the graveyard, gripping each others hands so tightly that they went numb. The moaning sound came from that steep part of the cemetery, and it was especially dark over there. Pearl's steps slowed a bit, and I guess she couldn't decide whether or not to venture on. Finally, we walked over to an open grave and strained to hear the sounds again.

Suddenly the moaning noises seemed to erupt violently from that open grave, and Pearl and I peered into it in panic. We caught a brief flash of movement down below but could not make out what it was. Pearl screamed "bloody-murder" and took off running. Her long legs enabled her to soar over the tombstones that blocked our path, while I stumbled along after her.

When we reached the little slope that led back to Aunt Polly's house, I lost my footing and rolled the rest of the way to the bottom, landing at Uncle Mick's feet. I guess he had heard our screams and decided to check things out.

"It's the end of the world!" Pearl gasped, breathless from running.

"The Dead is risin' up from their graves! The end of the world is here!"

Pearl then broke into a long, babbling dissertation of her many, many sins, begging the Lord's forgiveness and mercy.

Aunt Polly tried to compose her, but she would not be calmed. Uncle Mick steeled himself with a stiff shot of corn liquor and fetched down his old shotgun. For good measure, he ran to ask a neighbor-man to accompany him into the cemetery.

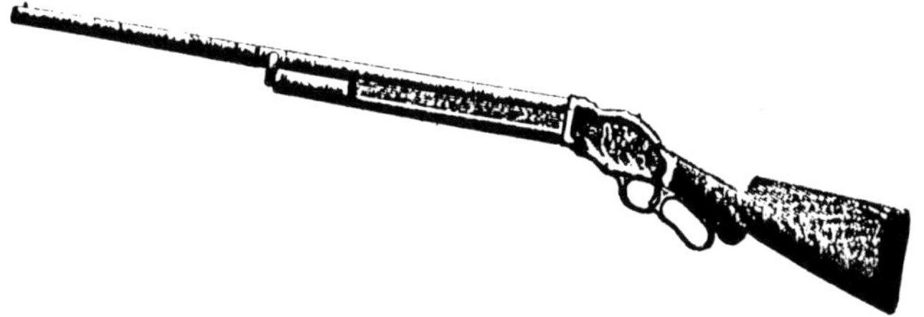

Much later that night, Mick returned. We found out that a neighbor's old horse had fallen into one of the open graves of the cemetery and had been trapped in there. It took Mick and his friend several hours to calm the poor animal down and to pull it out. Pearl felt a bit foolish about her hysterics, and tried to tell everyone she'd been joking. I knew better, though.

After that incident, Uncle Mick only dug graves as they were needed. Also, after that, Pearl and I were no longer required to fetch water after nightfall. That was an arrangement we were more than happy with.

CHAPTER III

BENNY BAKER

he summer of my eleventh year saw our family in dire need. Even the assistance of the local Salvation Army could not keep our heads above water. Just about the time we felt we had hit "rock-bottom", Daddy received a job offer. He was approached by a farmer, Mr. Baker, from St. Clement. Mr. Baker had been told Daddy was a fair carpenter, and he needed a man to do some building on his farm. We were provided a small cottage near the

Baker's farm house. All our worldly possessions
were piled high into the back of Daddy's old truck,
and Pearl and I rode atop the stack.

The Bakers were nice people, but they hadn't any
children my age to play with. From the very first,
I was bored with our new surroundings. I guess
Daddy saw my discontent, for he asked me to help

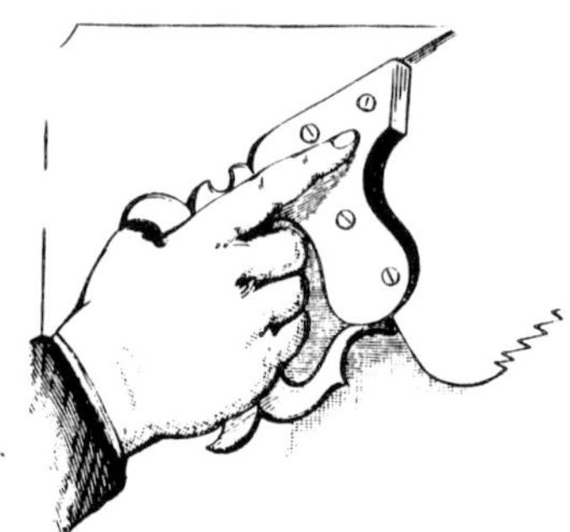

him out with his
job. I could fetch
him tools and nails
and the like, and
he would pay me
for the work. Just
being able to go
with Daddy would
have been enough

for me, but the prospect of getting a little money
didn't hurt either.

The next morning I accompanied him up to the
Baker's big farmhouse. Daddy had been instructed
to build a good-sized porch on the house, and he

already had it started. After
we had worked a few hours,
Mrs. Baker invited us into the
backyard for some lemon-
ade, and we readily accepted.

The first thing I saw when I rounded the corner
of the house was little Benny Baker. At first I didn't
notice his deformities. I was too engrossed in wat-
ching him wriggle and squirm to be free. He was
in a harness, and tethered to Mrs. Baker's clothesline with that harness.

When the boy spotted me, he withdrew to a small
bush nearby and then stared at me from beneath
it. I was aghast. I had never
witnessed mistreatment of a
child before, and I could not
take my eyes off little Benny.

I guess Mrs. Baker noticed my stare, and she laughed lightly.

"That there is my youngest boy, Benny." He ain't
right . . . never was, and defected, too."

I noticed, then, the malformed legs of little Benny.
His upper torso was almost perfectly formed, but
his legs were the size of an infant's, and he was
almost eight years old.

I noticed, too, his face. It was
like an angel's, framed by
golden curls and highlighted
by the brightest blue eyes I

had ever seen. Mrs. Baker went on to explain that Benny had been deformed since birth. He couldn't talk, other than in grunts and growls; and he was just plain "simple", as she put it. In order to keep him from wandering off, she had to tether him to the clothesline each day.

"I serve his meals outside, too, 'cause Benny eats with his fingers, and that way I don't have to clean up his messes from my clean floors."

 Benny finally came out from his hiding place beneath the bush, and half-crawled and half walked to a watering dish that lay on the ground. There, he lapped the water from the dish just like a dog would.

I shuddered a bit, more out of sympathy for his plight than anything else. Instinctively, I approached him with my hand extended in friendship. When he did not immediately withdraw, I stroked his golden curls and noticed again how beautiful his face was. He smiled at me. From that moment, Benny and I became very fast friends.

I made a point of spending most of my time with Benny, trying to ease his discomfort and boredom. I would sing to him and tell him stories and noticed how interested he seemed to be. For a child who had been termed a "complete idiot", Benny seemed to thoroughly understand the words I used. Even Daddy noticed that, and he laughed when Benny became upset about one of my story's unhappy endings. Then one day, as we sat on the lawn near where Benny was tied, eating our lunch, Daddy handed Benny a spoon. The little boy crawled over to his food-dish, and using the spoon as though he was quite accustomed to it, he ate his lunch.

Mrs. Baker was overjoyed at Benny's feat. After that, she encouraged him to use the utensil's at mealtime, and he became quite adept with the fork and spoon.

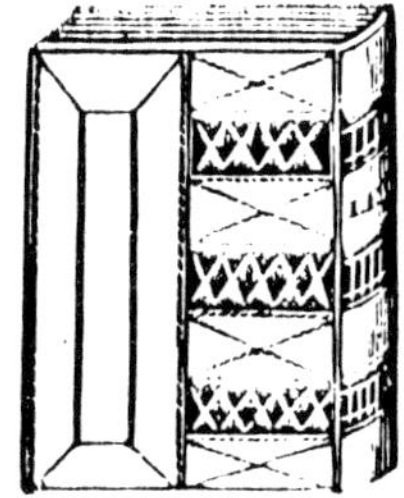

Another milestone in his improvement came one day when I visited him. On that particular day, I did not feel much like reading him his usual stories, so I sat in the shade next to him. He grunted meanly and motioned for me to open the book and get started. I just shook my head and stared off into space, totally absorbed in a daydream. Benny shook me slightly, but I ignored him. Then, I noticed him mouthing a word, and I quickly encouraged him.

"Read." he commanded. "Read."

I called for Daddy and Mrs. Baker, and Benny recited his first word to them. After that, Mrs. Baker asked that I try to spend more time with Benny, helping him to learn more words.

(37)

I agreed, for by that time, I sincerely loved little Benny.

Benny progressed rapidly. In no time at all, he had learned to talk, even though his speech was somewhat stilted, like a toddler's. His parents suddenly took a renewed interest in his development, and the clothesline tether was stored away.

Even Daddy, who was known for his soft heart, decided to help Benny along. In the evenings he  began work on a handcarved alphabet set for Benny. When the letters were finished, we painted each in a different color. I was the one appointed to give Benny this special gift, and he seemed delighted.

As he played with the letters, he began to recognize them among the words in my story books. He would happily point to an "A" or a "B", and I would applaud his new skill. By the end of the summer, Benny was putting letters together to form words. He had been able to print a bit and was quite proud of that achievement. His verbal skills greatly improved, too, and communication was no longer a problem for him.

That winter, while farm-chores had somewhat dwindled, Daddy found time to construct another gift for Benny. This time, he fashioned a hand-made wheelchair, perfectly pro-portioned for little Benny. We presented it to him on Christmas 

morning, and Benny cryed like a baby when he saw it. We had no idea how much freedom that wheelchair would afford him. Up until then, he had half crawled everywhere, and the going was slow and torturous. With the wheelchair, Benny was free to traverse the whole farm. It became his most cherished possession.

Though I argued that Benny should attend school for I felt he had amazing aptitude, his parents refused. There was still the problem of his terrible deformity, and they didn't want to submit him to the teasing and abuse his classmates would hand him. Benny remained at home, and I continued to tutor him until he had surpassed me.

Benny's father kept two small ponies on the farm, more for the enjoyment of his children than for any particular work.

When one of the ponies died, Daddy got an idea on how to use the remaining one. He worked feverishly to construct a small one-person pony cart for Benny. Benny's only limitation until then had been that he would get tired from wheeling his chair around. With a pony-cart, he would be free to travel at length and to his little heart's content.

Once again, the gift was tearfully and happily received. Benny immediately mastered leading his little pony about and often made a menace of himself and his cart on the county roads. He sped about constantly, quite often hindering the local traffic. He would allow me to ride on the back of the cart and sometimes would frighten me with his speed.

It was Benny's habit to go twice each day to the fields to deliver fresh water and a nice lunch to his father. I would accompany Benny, often clinging with white knuckles to the tiny cart as he sped along. Then one day, as we approached the pasture where Benny's father had been working, we noticed something was amiss.

In that particular pasture, Benny's father kept a mean old bull. That animal had been the cause of many a fright, for it was as mean-tempered as any bull we'd ever seen. We searched for the animal warily as we drove through the pasture gate. Benny began to call for his father,

worried suddenly that something had happened to him.

We drove the length of the pasture, and even Benny's little pony seemed uneasy. Then, we spotted the crumpled form of Benny's father laying beneath an oak tree near the fence-row. I leaped from the back of Benny's cart and raced to his father's side.

Mr. Baker was still. Blood seeped from a small wound on his temple, and I tried to shake him to consciousness. Meanwhile, Benny tried to maneuver the pony cart close enough to help.

Suddenly, we heard a low, rasping sound, and I immediately stiffened in fear. That sound was familiar to me . . . it was the noise Mr. Baker's bull made when it had been maddened. I stared across the pasture and saw the huge bulk of that animal bearing down on us. It had apparently been the cause of Mr. Baker's wound.

I screamed then and pointed in the direction of the charging bull. Benny whipped the  ny whipped the little pony forward quickly, and I thought, for a moment, that he was trying to flee. But then, he turned the cart deftly and made straight-away for the bull.

I watched with terror as the bull continued charging, not even slowing when it spotted Benny's tiny cart headed its way. At that moment, Mr. Baker sat up and rubbed his forehead a bit. He saw immediately what was going on, and he tried to get to his feet. The wounds he had sustained proved however, to be too much for him. He fell backwards against me, still too weak and dizzy to rise.

"Benny . . ." he called.

"Benny, don't . . . ."

Benny had maneuvered his little cart between the bull and us, and the crazed bull ran directly into it. I watched as the cart rolled on its side, throwing Benny roughly to the ground almost twenty feet away from it. The little pony, his eyes wide with fear, broke free and raced across the pasture to safety.

I must have fainted then, for the next thing I remembered is being carried in Daddy's arms back to our cottage. Daddy told me as he set me gently in bed that Benny had been killed. I couldn't believe it . . . my Benny, my bright, beautiful angel-faced little boy. He couldn't be dead, not after everything he'd been through. Daddy held me as I cried, and he cried, too.

Benny's funeral service was a blur to me. I couldn't bring myself to gaze into the coffin at his well-loved face. I remained, instead, seated in the back of the funeral home, quiet and pensive, and trying to recall the happy days I had spent with him.

Mrs. Baker came up to me afterwards and hugged me warmly. There were tears in her eyes as she thanked me. I guess she noticed my puzzled expression, and she went on to explain how I had been responsible for Benny's having a full and rich life . . . even though it had been a short one. That thought didn't provide me much comfort at the time, but now, years later, I know what Mrs. Baker meant.

For many years after that, I dreamed of one day having a child who looked like my Benny. My dream persisted, even though I knew the chances were quite slim. After all, I was dark-haired, so my children would most likely be the same. When my baby son was born, however, I was amazed. I stared with awe at the golden-blonde curls and bright blue eyes . . . and thanked God for the tiny angel-face that was so familiar to me.

CHAPTER IV

MABEL AND JESSE BROWN

e had just returned to Hannibal to live and had settled in one of the more poverty-strickened areas of town. Our home was tiny, run-down, and in an area of town commonly referred to as "The Bottoms". Most of the other houses on our street resembled ours, but the people who lived in them were goodhearted and friendly.

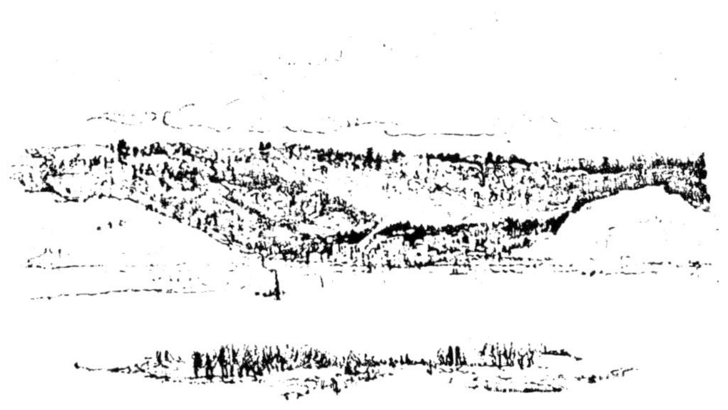

Our closest neighbors were a family of blacks, whose name was Brown. In those days, most black folks lived on the poor side of town, regardless of their wealth. Mabel and Jesse Brown seemed quite wealthy to us. They were the only family in the

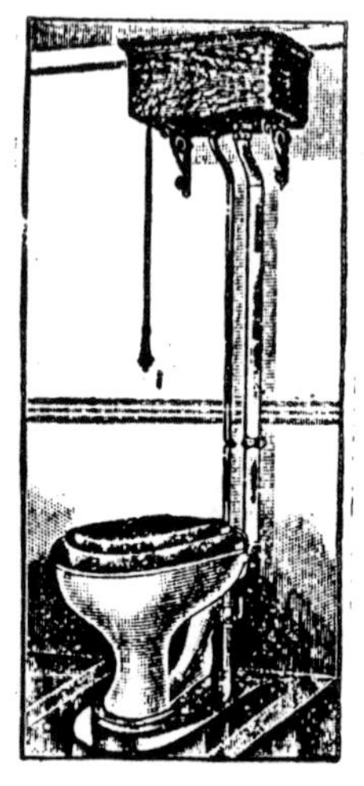

neighborhood who had indoor-plumbing, and it was a real source of interest. Jesse had his own car, and the garage it rested in was, by far, better than our humble house.

In spite of their wealth, the Browns were expected to treat white folks with a great deal of respect. My sisters and I were addressed by the title, "missie", by Mabel. They went out of their way to cater to us.

The Browns had two daughters, Hazel and Maggie. Hazel was my age, and Maggie was the baby. I loved to play with Hazel, for she had a fine collection of toys. Even she was required to address me

as "Missie Leona" during play. She usually complied, or at least did so when her mama was
around.

Mama Mabel must have been the prototype for
Aunt Jamima of syrup fame. Her huge bosom hung
well over the waist of her cotton dresses, and she
always wore a broad and sweet smile. She had the
blackest complexion I had ever seen, which made
her crisp white aprons appear even brighter.

Every day, Mabel would scrub her daughters in
the huge kitchen sink. I thought that was very odd
behavior, for we took baths only on Saturdays,
with a undue amount of ear scrubbin' in between.

My folks tolerated the Browns.
It was considered shameful to
be too social with colored folks,
but Momma and Daddy found
it hard to stay away. We would
often congregate in Mabel's
back yard and enjoy an easy

friendship. On occasion, Mabel and Jesse would wait on us hand and foot. Everyone, in fact, sort of took it for granted that they would.

Mamma Mabel became as protective and loving of us as she was of her own youngin's. She would deny her own daughters something, just so we could have our fill. That sort of treatment always puzzled me.

When Momma came down bad sick, it was Mabel who came to the rescue. She swept through our house like a tornado, clean-

ing and scrubbing it better than Momma ever had. Then, she proceeded to shuffle all of us kids back to her place. We spent several weeks in Mabel's tender care, so she could look after us while Momma recovered. I enjoyed her pampering and constant attention.

At mealtime, Mabel would seat us at the big wide table in her kitchen first, then fetch our plates and drinks until we were ready to burst. Her own family would be fed only after we had glutted ourselves. Even my Daddy, who had reservations about such treatment, was forced to eat his meal separately. Momma Mabel insisted that "it ain't fittin' nor proper for white folkses to be suppin' with darkies."

While in Mabel's care, my sisters and I succumbed to the daily baths. I began to enjoy being scrubbed

"squeaky-clean", but my younger sister's vehemently protested.

Often Hazel
and I would sit
on each side of
the large sink,
while Mabel
washed us in

the same water. I always wondered why the water
didn't turn black after Hazel's bath. On one occasion, I mentioned that fact to Mabel as she busily
bathed little Maggie.

"How do you tell when she's clean, Mama?" I asked innocently.

Mabel flashed me one of those big, warm smiles,
and laughed heartily.

"I jus' smells her, child," she replied.

"If'n she smells good, I'se done clennin'.

Far too soon, we moved from that quiet little
neighborhood and out of the lives of our friends,
the Browns. I learned a valuable lesson from Jesse
and Mabel, though, and one that I will never forget.
It matters very little what color a person's skin
might be or what he looks Like. What matters most
is the good he can do in this world.

CHAPTER V

THE OATLY LADY

s a youngster, I did not usually frighten easily. Even the prospect of a well-deserved whipping did not evoke, in me, the terror my siblings were prone to. But I can recall one occasion when I first tasted bone-chilling fear . . . the kind that can turn your hair white, and make your teeth chatter.

In those post-Depression days, my daddy would take almost any type of paying job he could find. So when approached with an offer to become a caretaker, he siezed it. Our family lived in a tiny apartment building on one of the biggest hills in town. Near the top of the hill, only a couple of blocks from us, stood an old abandoned mansion. It was the mansion Daddy had been hired to care for, even though the old place seemed beyond help. It had fallen to ruin through the years from neglect and vandalism, but I suppose its owners simply wanted to avoid further abuse.

Daddy made daily pilgrimages to the old house, and I accompained him. Once there, we set about cleaning the place as much as possible and boarding up some of the broken windows. It fascinated me to step into the spacious interior of that house. I always felt it necessary to catch my breath, for the place was much grander and more imposing than any house I'd ever seen.

I would ascend the great staircase as I had seen Theda Berra do in the picture shows . . . one hand gracefully extended to my imagined escort, bedecked with jewels and furs, and certainly "at home" in the fine mansion.

In between fetching washwater for Daddy, I explored the old place and could only imagine how grand it must have been when occupied by the Oatly family.

"Old man Oatly", as Daddy
called him, had been a
lumber magnate in Hannibal.
His intention was to build the
very finest home on the
river, and I felt he had suc-
ceeded. His three daughters
had been raised in the mansion, and I could only guess
at how pampered and lux-
urious their lives had been.

The Oatly daughters each
had her own suite of rooms,
while I shared a tiny room
with three sisters. The Oatly's had luxurious,
canopied, down-feather beds. I shared a bed with
three others, and my sister, Pearl, was forced to
sleep crossways at the foot.

It was common, in those days, for an abandoned
house to acquire a reputation for spooks and
haunts. The huge imposing Oatly Mansion was no
different, and all of the neighborhood children
feared it. Their accounts of terrible ghosts who in-
habited the place seemed humorous to me. After
all, I had explored the old mansion many times
and had never encountered anything other than
an occasional mouse or rat.

I had, however, never viewed the mansion at
night, when it loomed, huge and foreboding above
my frightened friends. Then one evening, I was
talked into accompanying some playmates to the
place after dark. Some of the boys in our crowd

told of the huge "bloody axe" they'd seen floating in the air in the house, and everyone was afraid . . . everyone, that is, but me. I laughed and scoffed, which proved to be my undoing.

I was immediately "dared" to enter the dark house. As proof of my bravery, I would be required to retrieve a lace curtain we could see in an upper story window.

Nothing to it, I thought. I had been in the room with that curtain many times before and could find my way there in the dark.

I did not count on just how dark and gloomy the old place was at night. When I hesitated at the front door, my friend's sudden burst of laughter urged me on. I had to do it; there was no turning back.

The only illumination in the mansion was dim moonlight that filtered through the dirty windows. I quickly found my way to the staircase and went to the upper floors. I was suddenly frightened by the echo of my own footsteps. In no time at all, however, I had found the room . . . and my prize. When I stepped to the window, I couldn't resist the urge to peer out at my friends on the

ground below. I waved bravely and was pleased
to hear their shouts of encouragement. I waved
the lace curtain in response.

I was suddenly filled with
reckless abandon, and felt
the impulse to climb up to
the Widow's Walk at the top
of the house. From that vantage point, my friends would
be greatly impressed with
my bravery. I imagined
myself to be a local hero, as
I climbed the narrow stair-

way, and I draped the tattered lace curtain about
my shoulders as if it were a fancy shawl.

I leaned far out over the
white-washed railing to get
my friends' attention, and
they cheered. I curtsied and
waved the lace curtain.

Then a movement from
nearby caught my eye.

I glanced over my
shoulder and was
surprised to find I was not alone on the Widow's
Walk. Only slightly taller than me, a middle-aged
lady stood very close by. Her gown was quite old-
fashioned, and it rustled slightly as she approached the rail. She seemed oblivious to my presence
and simply fixed her glaze on the horizon. I tried
to see what had attracted her attention, but saw

only the gentle curve of the Mississippi River as it snaked about the bluffs at the edge of town. When I turned to the lady once more, she had vanished.

When the realization finally sunk in that I had witnessed an apparition, I screamed. It took only seconds to find my way out of the mansion and back to my friends. My skinny legs carried me faster than they ever had before.

My playmates needed no explanation, for my white face and the speed with which I hurled myself past them told them something was amiss. They joined me in flight, and we didn't stop running until we had reached the relative safety of the school-yard. There, I sank, exhausted and breathless, into the dew-soaked grass. My sister, Gracie, could not contain her curiousity and insisted that I tell everything.

Still shivering with fear, I related the whole story, providing a detailed description of the ghostly lady I had seen. My friends sat, wide-eyed, in a circle about me as I colored the story a bit to hold their interest.

Weeks later, I was pleased to find my account of the Oatly Lady-Ghost had taken complete precedence over the "bloody-axe" story. My en-

counter was recited over and over, and some of
the story-tellers added a bit of flavor to enliven the
account.

Daddy seemed a bit disturbed at my reluctance to
return to the mansion with him after that, but he
finally excused me from the chore. My sister, Pearl,
accompanied him instead. Pearl held the opinion
that, between her and Daddy, no spook had half
a chance. I guess she was right, for they never
were bothered by the mansion's ghosts.

I've been told the whole thing was a product of
my young imagination. Years later, though, I still
vividly recall the Oatly Lady, and the sadness in
her eyes as she stared at the river. I can sympathize
with her a bit . . . had I been afforded a chance
to dwell in that beautiful mansion - alive or dead
- I would have done so, too.

CHAPTER VI

HALF PINT HOBO

s a young girl, I was fascinated with the hobos and railroad bums who drifted into and out of our town. I explored their encampments with great interest, often finding the remains of a hurriedly-consumed meal and a still-smouldering campfire. To me, eating one's dinner from a can seemed sheer luxury, and I dreamed of reclining by an open fire to await the

call of a passing locomotive. Hobos were the epitome of the "free spirit", and I much envied the ragged dirty "railway gentleman". I did not know I would soon join their ranks.

My sister, Pearl, at four years my senior, was a free spirit, too. She often ignored the commands of our parents and would shrug off even the most brutal of whippings. She scoffed at the neighborhood bullies, and she could cuss better and longer than anyone I'd ever seen.

Most of the time Pearl tolerated me quite well, but there were times when my pestering and nagging would test the limits of her endurance. One such time was a bright summer afternoon, when I followed Pearl down our street.

I knew she was impatient to be rid of me, so I stayed well out of reach of her fist. I even began  to tease her a bit, knowing full well she was quickly becoming enraged. When she had finally had enough of my tormenting, she turned and shoved me roughly.

"Git on home, now, Lee", she commanded. "Or I'll have to hurt you!"

My feelings were hurt. Of all my sisters, Pearl had always been protective and loving of me. Her sudden dislike of my company would not go unpunished. I stuck my tongue out at her, still maintaining my distance just out of reach and tried to summon a real good cuss-word. Pearl took a step toward me, and I stumbled backwards. In the fall, I had managed to dirty my fresh smock, and my knee had gotten pretty well skinned-up.

Pearl was instantly filled with remorse. She knelt down beside me, and consoled me as much as possible. When she was sure I wasn't hurt badly, however, she jerked me back to my feet.

"Now, didn't I tell you," she shouted, "To git fer home?"

With that she smacked my behind lightly, sending me scurrying back down the road.

I was humiliated and angry, and by the time I reached our house, I had contrived a way to "get even" with Pearl.

Momma was duly sympathetic when she saw my bloody knee, and when I described how Pearl had slapped my behind. I proceeded to tell her that Pearl had also knocked me down, dirtying my smock in the process. Though Momma knew I could sometimes be a pest to Pearl, she agreed Pearl's punishment had far exceeded the crime.

When Pearl finally returned home that day, Momma met her at the door with the

hickory-switch. I was well familiar with the pain that switch could inflict, and I winced a bit as it was brought down across Pearl's behind.

Pearl, being brave and hardheaded, never cried during a whipping, which only meant that her beatings were much more prolonged and brutal. I had never "told" on anyone before, and I felt like an ogre. When Momma raised the switch to strike again, I shouted for her to stop. In tears, I poured out a confession and begged forgiveness for the lie I had concocted.

With some relief, I watched Momma replace the switch in its storage spot. She turned to me, her face red with anger, and shook her finger only a few inches from my nose.

"I will not abide . . . ", she shouted;" . . . a dirty little liar!"

With that, she said what I had dreaded to hear;

"You will have no supper tonight, child . . . now, git to yer room!"

I climbed the steps to my loft-bedroom quickly, sure at any moment Momma would flail me. Pearl followed and tried to console me a bit as I cried.

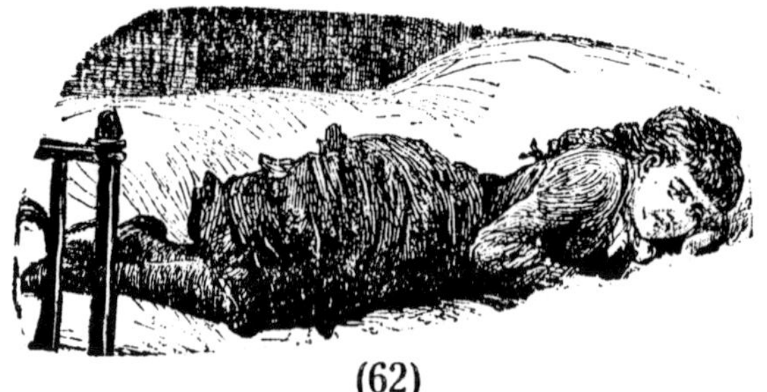

Momma related every detail of the incident to Daddy as soon as he got home from work. In a very soft voice, he summoned me from my room and ordered me to be seated. He told me how disappointed he was in me, and I began to cry. Then he devised what he felt to be a fitting punishment for my lie. I would remain at home for a whole week, and Momma would provide me with chores to keep me occupied and "out of trouble". I began to cry even harder. My father's sudden cruel streak puzzled me. He knew full well what being confined at home with Momma meant. My mother, beloved as she was, would have made any Gestapo commander proud.

In a sudden burst of temper, I announced I was leaving home. I waited for my parents' reaction, which I supposed would be panic.

Daddy only calmly sat there, and then suggested that I at least stay for supper, seeing as how it might be my last decent meal for a while. I reluctantly agreed, infuriated by his uncaring attitude.

Returning to my room, I gathered my most prized possessions into an old handkerchief. There was a nice cat-eye marble I had found, a buckeye, two pretty rocks, and a nearly-new fish hook.

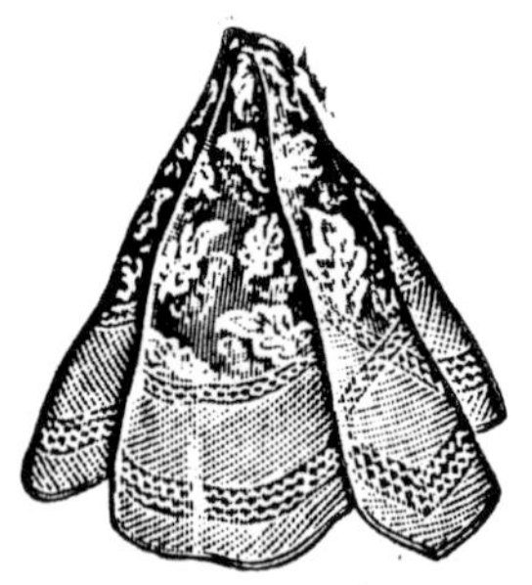I tied the handkerchief in a knot and slung it over my shoulder.

Pearl, all the while, pleaded with me to reconsider. She was in tears when we descended the stairs to the kitchen. Daddy sat at the table, still smoking his pipe and reading the newspaper.

"Didn't forget anything, did you, Hon?", he asked politely.

I shook my head, sincerely wishing he wouldn't be so darned glad to see me go. I was far too stubborn to tell him so, though.

When Pearl begged me once more to stay, Daddy interrupted her.

"Now, Lonie-girl knows what she wants, So you jus let her be."

I didn't see the wink he shot to Pearl.

After supper, which I lingered over much longer than usual, I rose and said my goodbyes. Slinging the handkerchief back over my shoulder, I stepped out the back door and into the darkness. I knew exactly where I wanted to go, 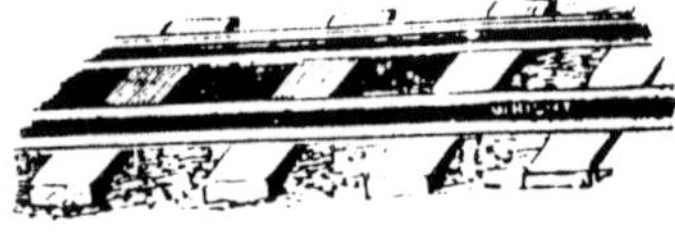and I made my way there methodically.

In no time at all I reached the old railroad switch yards. The place seemed abandoned, and it was very very dark. Unbeknownst to me, Daddy had ordered Pearl to follow and fetch me home "as soon as I got scared." Daddy hadn't counted on just how brave, or how stubborn, I really was. Pearl

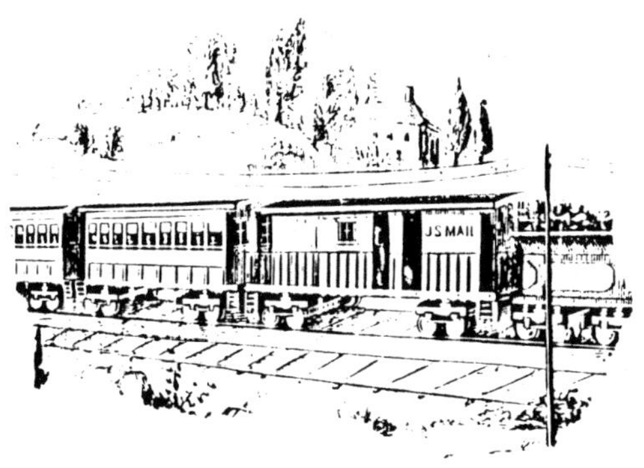

hid in some bushes, wondering why I had traveled so far from home.

The shadow of a long train loomed nearby, and I headed for it. The train had stopped in the switch-yard, and I was afforded an opportunity to "shop" for the boxcar I would ride in. I walked the length of the train, peering into open cars, until I had pick-ed one that looked a little cleaner and more in-viting. I climbed into it carefully, and stood up in the doorway. I was quite proud of myself. At that moment, I spotted Pearl moving toward me across the yards.

Also, at that moment, the train lurched forward suddenly, throwing me roughly to the floor. By the time I was able to pull myself back to my feet, the train was moving steadily, picking up speed as it

went, I clung to the door for dear life and saw
Pearl's nimble figure racing along after the train.
Pearl was the best runner in our neighborhood,
and she began to gain on my freight car.

"Jump, Lonie-girl, jump!"

The scenery seemed to be whizzing by, and my
stomach had started to churn. I shook my head,
"No" and clung to the door with white knuckles.

In a super-human leap, Pearl dove into the box car
at my feet. Once more she commanded me to
jump, and once more, I vehemently refused.

Pearl pryed my fingers loose from the death-drip
I had on the door. Then cradling me against her,
she leaped out of the boxcar.

We landed on a very rough gravel embankment
and tumbled down it into a mud puddle. When we
were finally still, I found myself still in Pearl's
embrace.

I was unhurt, but she seemed bruised and scratched from head to toe.

"You okay, Lee?"

I nodded and hugged her tightly. At that moment, Pearl seemed to be the bravest and most perfect sister in the whole world.

On our way home, Pearl asked me not to tell our folks about the train ride. She figured, and rightly so, that they would probably never let us out of sight again after hearing about the incident.

I had learned a very valuable lesson that night and was pleased when Momma and Daddy welcomed me back home with open arms. I never fantasized about a hobo's life again, nor did I ever feel compelled to become one.

CHAPTER VII

THE DEVILISH ANGEL

uring the long Missouri winters, it was common for my family to suffer frequent colds and influenza. It always seemed like we passed the germs around to one another and were constantly fighting some type of virus. Momma's sure-fire remedy for our ailments was always a shot of patent medicine or a stiff dose of castor-oil, laced with cooking sherry. Even though the remedy often failed to effect a cure, we'd do just about anything to avoid another dose. Momma's doctoring, or even the threat of it, usually saw us back on our feet in no time at all.

There was one time, however, when even Momma could not stir my recovery. My influenza symptoms, persisted far longer than they should have, and the daily doses of castor-oil only served to make me sicker. My folks became very concerned one evening when my temperature sky-rocketed. I overhead Momma make the decision that Doctor Grant should be summoned.

I had never been treated by a real doctor before, and the prospect of it frightened me. I had heard all the horror stories my friends had concocted about Doctor Grant and could only imagine what sort of suffering the old man might inflict on me. Dizzy and weak, I managed to crawl from my warm bed. The only thing to do, in my opinion, was to hide from the doctor. Surely, he would give up and leave when I couldn't be found.

I chose a hiding place in one corner of our tool-shed. There was coal-bin there, and I paid little attention to the black powder that clung to my bare

legs. Snow sifted through cracks in the wooden sides of the shed, and I shivered so violently my teeth chattered.

My plan failed miserably, for Daddy found me right away. I was far to weak to argue and was glad for the warmth of our house. The doctor's brief diagnosis was "pneumonia", and he insisted that I be taken to the hospital.

Doc Grant had a two-seater coupe, and I was bundl-
ed up and placed in it. I can still recall the very
worried looks my parents wore as they carried me
to his car.

There would be no room for them to accompany
us to the hospital, but Daddy assured me he would
try to get there quickly.

He convinced a neighbor to drive him to within
a few blocks of the hospital, and he walked the
rest of the way through the bitter cold and snow.

Meanwhile, it was decided that the coal-dust had to be washed off me. I didn't have the strength to sit up, so one nurse had to hold me while the other scrubbed, They then placed me in a small bed that resembled a crib. It angered me to think I was being treated like a baby, and I tried to protest. The nurse seemed to care very little that my feelings had been hurt, and simply went about her work.

I do not recall Daddy's visit but was told later he spent several hours at my bedside. Doc's prognosis about my condition was quite grim. He tenderly informed Daddy that it would be a miracle if I survived the night. On hearing that news, my usually  sober and responsible father went out to a bar and got completely drunk. The next morning some friends dumped him back on Momma's front porch, and he had to be carried inside.

That night at the hospital was a blur of activity. Nurses and doctors alike constantly hovered over me, fussing with medication, thermometers, and such. I slept fitfully, often waking to see my unfamiliar surroundings. At one point during the night, I awoke feeling a bit refreshed.

The room was very dark and for once I was alone there. I fixed my gaze on the ceiling, trying to recall the events of the day. Suddenly, a slight movement from nearby caught my attention.

I heard a very familiar giggle, and recognized it

immediately as Lily's laugh. She hovered a few feet over my bed, seemingly suspended in mid-air. Her garb resembled that of an angel's, complete with wings, and she smiled happily at me as she flew about in a circle.

I knew Lilly better than anyone else, and I knew for a fact she was anything but an angel. Her constant moaning and pestering of me could be quite devilish at times.

Her appearance over my hospital bed infuriated me, for I was sure she had come to taunt and tease. I shouted at her to stop flying about, but she ignored me. Then I sat up, and shook a first at her. Lily continued her erratic flight above my bed. When I tried to slap her, she eluded me expertly. I shouted at her again and felt someone's hand on my shoulder.

I turned with a start to see Doc Grant sitting on the edge of my "crib". He smiled at me and took my temperature.

"Much better today, Leona."

He was right; I did feel better. I was suddenly very hungry. I tried to describe Lily's strange visit to Doctor Grant, but he only laughed.

My recovery was rapid, and I was able to return home shortly after that. I told Momma about Lily-The-Angel having visited me, and she took it as a sign from God. She believed in the vision and that I had seen an angel, but I had very serious doubts. Lily was anything but angelic, so why would a real angel take her form?

CHAPTER VIII

BANANAS

ear Hannibal's river-front area, there stood a huge three-story brick and stone structure called The Gossard Grocery Company. I remember the name well, for it was painted on the side of the building in yard-high letters. That place was a regular summertime stop for me. It seemed the foolish folks who ran it liked to dispose of perfectly good fruit from time to

time, and I would often rummage through it. The overripe bananas and oranges were exotic delicacies to me, for my only taste of them otherwise was at Christmastime when the Salvation Army would hand them out.

One day when there wasn't much to choose from in the "trash" pile, I noticed the huge door to the building was open. This was very unusual, and my curiosity was piqued. I had imagined all sort of strange things going on inside that building and just had to investigate. Perhaps, in there, I would find the foreign trees that grew the delicious fruits.

I went into the building steathily, ever wary of being "caught" by someone. Though the ground floor seemed vacant, I could hear voices from the upper stories.

The building was not at all what I had imagined. Instead of the tropical rainforest I expected, it  looked much like a warehouse. The walls were lined with stacks of bags and barrels. I was disappointed and felt like leaving for a moment. But, then, I noticed another doorway at the end of the big room. The floor in that area sloped down sharply, and the doorway led to what I thought must be a basement area.

Prompting my decision to investigate further was the fact that the voices had descended to the stairway by then. I could either race for the exit or hide and hope for the best. The pungent aroma of bananas hung heavy in the air as I raced through that "basement" doorway. I strained in the darkness for a glimpse of the much-sought-after bananas. Sure enough, near the bottom of the ramp, crates were overflowing with green bananas.

I ran from one crate to another, sampling from each as I did so and filling my pockets full of the fruit. I was in "hog-heaven", and wondered just how many bananas I could make off

with. When I heard the footsteps approaching from the main floor, I panicked.

The banana crates did not afford a decent hiding-place, so I plummeted further into the "basement". The steeply-sloping ramp resembled a tunnel, and it seemed to have no end. Still, I felt that at any moment, I would see sunlight streaming through an exit up ahead. As I ran along, I encountered only more darkness.

It was pretty chilly in the tunnel, and the walls were damp and slimy. I shivered a little, thinking this place was quite a lot more frightening than any cave or haunted-house I'd ever been in. I began to wonder how I would find my way back out of there, for I had lost sight of the pathway I had taken.

Exhausted from running, I sat down on the damp tunnel floor to catch my breath. Suddenly, I imagined huge, hairy rats moving about in the darkness. It seemed only natural that rodents, snakes, and the like would inhabit such a spooky place, and I formed a mental picture of rats gnashing their teeth at me. Course, I reckoned the boa-constrictors would probably beat the rats out of their "easy meal", and that thought provoked me to start running again.

I bumped into the slimy walls, into crates, and barrels. I stumbled around in the darkness for what 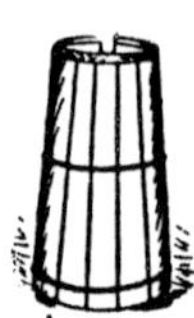seemed an eternity. When, at last, I found the doorway again, I didn't care if someone caught me or not, as long as it wasn't a rodent or a snake.

I scrambled up the slippery ramp and out the door as though my skirt-tail was on fire, flinging bananas with every step. The hot sunshine felt wonderful, and I silently thanked God for my deliverance from the depths of the The Grocer Company.

By the time I reached home, there was only one tiny, green banana left in my pocket. Though I felt sure it could probably be traded to one of my sisters for something of great value, I tossed it to

(78)

the ground with some dis-
dain and mashed it with my
bare foot.

Many years later, I found out
that the spooky tunnel I had
explored served a very
useful purpose for The Grocery Company. Unripen-
ed fruit could be stored in its chilly depths for long
periods of time.

The tunnel was even said to extend far under the
Mississippi River, and I'm sure I didn't get that far.

To this day, I gag at the thought of eating bananas.

CHAPTER IX

THE EVICTION

ur lodgings were seldom what one would consider luxurious and comfortable. In fact, there were times when we wondered if Daddy would be able to provide housing of any kind. We usually lived in those sections of town where the "eviction process" was a common occurrence, and we feared it might happen to us, Fortunately, our landlords were usually

understanding and patient, and Daddy could plead our cases successfully. There were other landlords, however, who seemed to enjoy evictions and would conduct the procedure personally with little regard for the poor tenant.

One such landlord was Harrison Hynds. He owned many of the dwellings in our neighborhood and
was not a bit tolerant of the misfortunes of his
tenants. Mr. Hynd's evictions usually came with
little warning, even though the tenant was fully
aware of rent pastdue. I suppose the tenant hoped
- - - to the last - - - that Mr. Hynds would be merciful
and understanding. That's why Mr. Hynd's evicted
tenants always seemed shocked and aghast when
the police showed up at their doorstep.

Evictions were a terrible ordeal, both for the tenant
and the entire neighborhood. The family's personal

belongings would be
toted out to the street
by grim police of-
ficers while Mr.
Hynds supervised.
Many times the peo-
ple themselves had to
be toted, or dragged,
out to the curb also.

While friends and neighbors gathered to dispense
the unfortunate family's belongings to shelter, we

hotly discussed Mr.
Hynd's cruelty. The
family would usually
be taken in by so-
meone, even though
it often meant tem-
porary separation for
the larger families.
Folks, in general,

would do everything possible to help the homeless family get "back on their feet". In the meantime, Mr. Hynes did not allow his property to stand vacant. There was a steady stream of tenants for his dwellings.

Mr. Hynd's evictions, though swift and cruel, were well within the law. Though we knew full well the unlucky tenant's struggle for survival, we were also aware of his failure to pay Mr. Hynd's rent. Nothing could be done, other than to grumble and to curse the "fate of the poor". There was one occasion, however, when Mr. Hynd's cruelty seemed vastly unjust, and the whole neighborhood turned out to plead with him.

Near the end of our street, Birdie and Ida Yohnt lived in a modest little home. They were the unofficial grandparents of the neighborhood, and had more patience with youngins than anyone else I knew. Ida often carried food and medicine to the quarantined families and could be counted on to help when one needed it.

Birdie was a retired railroad engineer, a fact I found quite glamorous. He had been injured in what he called "The Shortline Derailment", and was left with a very pronounced limp. The other children and I would gather around Birdie to hear his tales of railroading while Ida prepared shortbread cookies and punch. Though they were far from wealthy, Birdie's modest pension kept their heads above water.

Birdie occasionally mentioned his "savings", but a stern look from Ida would abruptly end that topic of conversations.

It seems that, before Birdie and Ida moved to our neighborhood, they had a fine house in one of the town's wealthier districts. During his career in railroading, Birdie had set aside a nest egg to see them through their retirement. When I inquired of Birdie what had happened to his life's savings, his face became grave and drawn.

"Stolen", he muttered.

"Ever' penny took by a thievin' scallawag."

I found out much later that the "Scallawag" Birdie spoke of was, in fact, his own son. Though I never knew the circumstances surrounding the theft, I knew that Birdie had ordered the boy out of the house, and out of his life, forever. Ida kept a framed picture of the boy on her mantle and would often gaze at it longingly. But the boy's name could not be mentioned in Birdie's house; he would not allow it.

Ida did stay in touch with her son. In fact, she saw him every week. After his father had "tossed the poor lad out", Ida found him an apartment in a neighboring block. In charge of their budget, Ida would somehow manage to secrete the funds for her son's board and room. Every Tuesday, she was off to market or so she told Birdie. Instead, she would rush over to her son's apartment, cleaning and stocking it for the week ahead. We would watch with some amusement as she fairly raced through the small general store, buying a few groceries for herself to "make it look good". Birdie often complained that his money didn't go very far, and I wondered if he suspected Ida's secret.

The strain of keeping two households began to show. Ida was no longer able to offer the neighbor children cookies and punch. She did keep a small supply of hard-candy for special occasions. She began to sell a few personal belongings, of course without letting Birdie know, and her neighbors began to worry. Paying her son's living expenses had put quite a strain on her own meager budget, and Birdie began to complain that there was never enough to eat.

I suppose it came as no surprise, the day Harrison Hynd's big automobile parked in front of Ida's house. It was a bitter cold day, and the rain had begun to fall. As Momma and I huddled together beneath our umbrella on the way home from the general store, she paused by Ida's gate. I had taken little notice of Mr. Hynd's car parked on the street, but the two police cars parked behind it sparked my interest.

One of the officers tipped his hat and spoke to Momma, but she did not reply. Instead, she rushed over to Ida's neighbor's house, admonishing me to wait by the gate. Very soon, Momma returned. The "alarm" had been sounded, and neighbors from both ends of our street came running, clutching umbrellas and raincoats. We gathered and waited by Ida's gate, hoping to offer some comfort, I suppose.

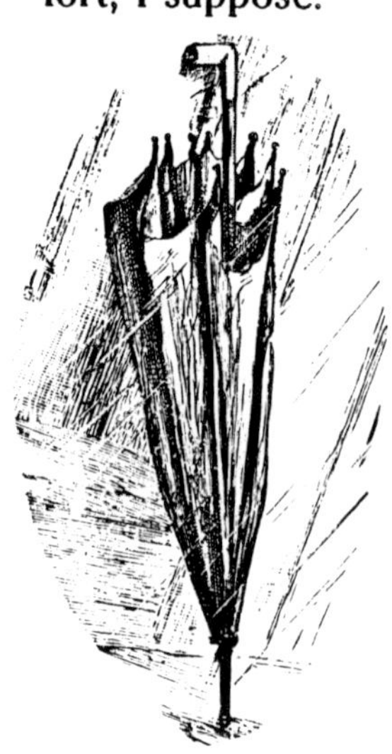

Birdie's voice sounded strained as he ordered Mr. Hynd "off the premises."

Ida began to sob pitifully, and then pleaded with her landlord.

"One more day . . . . . ." she cried;

"I'm sure we kin raise the money . . . please!"

Mr. Hynds merely brushed past her and began to carry furniture out into the street. With their front door wide open, we could see Birdie sinking tiredly into his easy-chair. He was shaking his  head in disbelief, and then staring at Ida imploringly.

The officers completed their grueling task, and most of the Yohnt's possessions became wringing wet. A few of us began to carry the things to shelter. Someone volunteered to store the heavier items in his shed, and the menfolk rushed to do the task. Ida seemed dazed, and Momma tried to console her.

"You will stay with us, now", Momma whispered. "I insist."

Ida simply nodded, and mumbled a soft thank you.

Birdie refused to be moved. He remained in his easy-chair and would not allow the officers to pull him from it. Finally, two of them picked Birdie up, chair and all, and carried him out into the rain.

Satisfied with the work, Mr. Hynds got into his car

and drove away . . . splattering mud on Ida's daven-
port as he did so.

Ida accompanied us home, but Birdie refused to
leave. He chose, instead, to remain in his easy-chair
in the pouring rain. Someone covered him with
a raincoat, and he stayed there for over two hours.
When Daddy finally convinced him to leave, he
had to have help making the short walk to our
house.

I suppose Birdie had given a great deal of thought
to his predicament and had guessed at Ida's decep-
tion. He had no sooner entered our house when
he began to shout at her.

"You and that damned boy!" he said as he pointed
a shaking finger at
her.

"Steal me blind . . . .
. . take everything . .
. even my home!"

Ida said nothing. She simply cried softly and wrung
her hands.

Our tiny house didn't afford much room, and even
our own family was cramped. Still, we tried to
make Birdie and Ida feel comfortable and
welcome. Daddy told them they could stay with
us as long as necessary, knowing full well we could
not afford to feed the extra mouths.

I suppose, from his stubborn refusal to come in out

of the rain, Birdie became very ill. By the next morning, he had a high fever, and could not leave his bed. Ida was frantic with worry, for Birdie refused food and drink. He withdrew into himself, refusing to speak to anyone. Ida tried to explain things to us.

"Birdie has always been a proud man; proud that he stood on his own two feet."

We could all see that to be evicted and at the mercy of neighbors was a powerful blow to his ego.

Ida went to visit her son that week and explained what had happened. I suppose the boy felt a sense of remorse at his parent's plight, because he returned with her to see his father.

Birdie, however, adamantly refushed to see his son. He became so agitated at the sight of him, in fact, that Ida feared he would have a stroke. She stayed in Birdie's room, to calm him down a bit, while the boy sat dejectedly in our kitchen. He seemed a likeable sort, and I felt sorry for him. His name was Royce, and he told us, too, that he was unaware of his father's financial straits. His mother had always assured him they were managing quite well. He told us he would provide shelter for his parents and planned to take them back to his apartment to live. By the time we had gotten to know Royce better, we began to wonder how such a nice person could have done the things Birdie accused him of.

In his weakened state, there was little Birdie could do to avoid being transported to Royce's apartment. Before leaving our house, Royce entered his father's room to talk to him.

By then, the old man had calmed down a lot and there wasn't the shouting he had done earlier. Royce was in the room for quite a while with his mother and father. When he came out, he told us that they had had a good talk and that his father was now ready to leave.

Daddy offered to help move the old man, and another neighbor volunteered the use of his coalwagon.

Daddy told us later that, as they drove to Royce's apartment, Birdie asked them to stop at the house he and Ida had rented. He stared at the empty dwelling with tears in his eyes and held Ida's hand tightly.

When Royce embraced the old man, he didn't push him away. Instead, he seemed glad for the affection and comfort of his son.

It's only a house," Birdie whispered. "It isn't even a very nice house at that . . . . and not nearly big enough for the three of us, anyway."

CHAPTER X

TAVERN-TRICK

e lived in an upstairs apartment on South Main Street for several years. Only three doors down from our building, one of the most popular taverns in town stood, and it was a source of some contention between my parents. Every evening after work, Daddy and a few of his coworkers would stop at the tavern on their way home.

They never drank too much beer, but the fact that they stopped at all aggravated Momma to no end. She would try to keep Daddy's supper warm until he made it home but quite often burned it in the process. 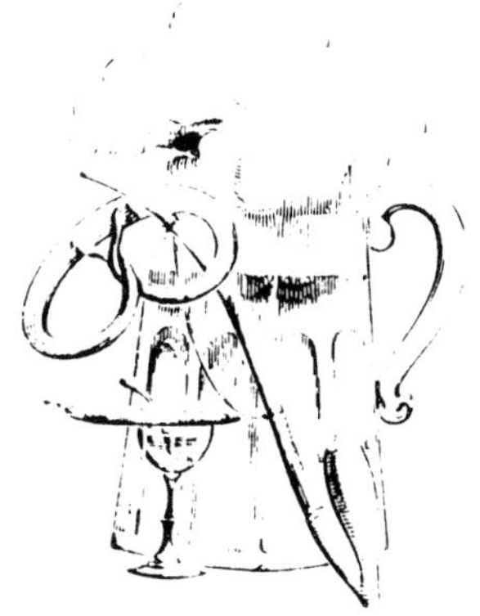
The spoiled suppers were of little consequence to

her, though. What concerned her most was the terrible influence that tavern might have on Daddy. She imagined all sorts of low-lives and thieves hanging out in there and was certain Daddy would pick up their nasty habits.

After several months of worry and fear, she decided to do something about the situation. Summoning Pearl and me into the kitchen, she sat us down and told us her plan. With our help, Daddy would no longer have the desire to visit the tavern.

In a faint whisper, she explained how we were going to help.

"You two youngins are gonna go on down to that tavern. And when you git in, you go find yer Daddy, hear?"

We nodded, a little excited that we were finally going to see the terrible tavern with all those low-lives.

"You jus' sit yourselves down next to 'im, and start whinin' and naggin' 'bout how hungry you-all are."

Pearl and I were puzzled. We had just eaten and weren't hungry at that particular time.

As if reading our thoughts, Momma continued her plot.

"You just let on like you're hungry, and nag and complain how you ain't et anything all day . . . thataway, your poppa will be real embarrassed and come right on home with you."

We had to giggle a bit at Momma's genius, and we happily set off for the tavern within a few minutes.

After our eyes had grown accustomed to the darkness of the place, we spotted Daddy at the end of a long polished bar. He was in conversation with a man so we took a seat next to him and remained quiet for a while. As soon as there was a lull in the conversation, Pearl tugged on his shirt-sleeve roughly.

"Daddy." she moaned in a loud voice. "I'm just a-starvin'!"

I copied Pearl's actions, grabbing my stomach and moaning slightly. At the same time, we had to stifle the giggles.

Daddy seemed taken aback by Pearl's pronounce-
ment so she repeated it. This time, the whole bar
heard how "hungry and starving" we were, and
how we hadn't had a bite of food all day.

Daddy's face got red and I
noticed all the looks he got
from the other patrons.
Without a word to anyone,
he got up and walked out.
Pearl and I followed him
home, skipping and laughing
all the way.

Momma's plan had worked
so well, and we knew she
would reward us for our
good work. Daddy never
mentioned the incident to us,
but we heard the heated
discussion he had with Momma later that night.
Momma would not relent; she wanted him out of
the tavern for good, and she told him she would
do it even if it took her children to help.

I suppose I inherited my stubbornness from Daddy,
for he just plain wouldn't give up the tavern . . .
to spite Momma, I guess. It became our daily task
to follow him there, and perform our "hungry" act.

Daddy's acquaintances soon caught on to our trick,
and it became a source of amusement. Daddy,
however, became tired of it, and he would often
dispatch us back home with the threat of a whipping. Finally, he devised a way to put a stop to

the antics . . . and to teach Momma a good lesson at the same time.

Though it was unusual for Daddy to attend church with us, he did so that Sunday morning. He even paused after the service to socialize with some of Momma's friends.

Only I knew the nature of that conversation with them, and I was sworn to secrecy about it.

Daddy "accidently" mentioned the fact that Momma had been sending her daughters down to that terrible tavern every day. The lady he talked to was properly shocked and amazed and pumped him for more information.

"I reckon," Daddy calmly replied; "She just wants them youngin's outta her hair for a while, and that tavern is the only place she can find to send them to."

Daddy smiled as we walked home from church, secure in the knowledge that the terrible rumors about Momma were spreading like wild fires. He wasn't disappointed, for the very next day, the misguided gossip reached Momma's ears.

She nearly died of embarrassment when Aunt Beth related the story. No one could seem to recall where the ugly gossip had gotten its start, but

Momma was suddenly ashamed to show her face
in public. Aunt Beth had been told, in fact, that
Momma was forcing us to work at the tavern, per-
forming exotic dances for the men.

We were no longer sent to embarrass my father
after that, for Momma didn't feel like fueling the
fires of gossip any more. But then, there was no
longer a need to visit Daddy at the bar, for he
became quite punctual about returning home.

CHAPTER XI

"SLIPPERY" AND "STEW"

uring the time we lived in Benbow, Daddy spent most of his time away from home. His job in Peoria required far too much travel for frequent trips home. He did, however, manage to visit us now and then. Money was scarce, so Daddy relied on the occasional empty boxcar of the railways for transportation. In those days, it was common for folks to "catch" a ride on a passing train. Though the engineer and switchmen tolerated their unexpected passengers quite well, the railroad didn't much like the "free-riders". They would dispatch teams of inspectors and guards to check their lines and evict the hobos.

Daddy described the railway guards as burly brutes who delighted in inflicting as much pain as they could on those they caught. They would whip their prey with chains and clubs so survival for a hobo meant keeping a wary eye open at all times, lest they get caught by one of those men.

Daddy learned much from the hobos. He talked enthusiastically about their camaraderie and the warm welcomes he received in hobo-camps. Many a kind-hearted hobo shared his meager meal with my Daddy, and Daddy learned the tricks of riding the rails from them. He learned, too, the recipe for Mulligan Stew and became famous along the line for his expertise at that dish.

Though Daddy had always made it a practice to spend our birthdays at home with us, that year we had given up hope that he would make it home for Betsy's fifth birthday. We were thankful, at least, that he had managed to spend Christmas with us. Betsy, however, was too young to understand. She looked forward to Daddy's arrival and to the rock-candy he always brought with him. I suppose Daddy felt guilty about missing Betsy's "big day," for he was determined to make it home . . . and nothing Momma could say would change his mind.

He bought the required rock-candy in Peoria and then caught a south-bound train. Daddy's trips home were always filled with danger, but they had their enjoyable moments, too. By that time, he was familiar with the many hobo camps along the track and knew most of the patrons of those camps. The hobos gave Daddy the nickname "Stew", because of his skill at making that Mulligan Stew. At each hobo camp someone always knew of Daddy's reputation as a cook and would ask him to prepare a meal.

On the first night of his trip home for Betsy's birthday, Daddy camped beneath a trestle. A large gathering of hobos was there, and he was required to prepare the stew. A scavenger hunt was formed for the stew ingredients, and each hobo dutifully added an ingredient to the pot.

With full bellies, the men then sat around their campfire and laughed. Daddy was induced to "play a lick or two" on his harmonica, and the others joined in with

makeshift instruments. With a warm fire and the night sky for a ceiling, those hobos seemed a fortunate lot, indeed. They did have cause for suffering, however, and most had horror stories about how the Depression had wiped them out and how they had lost their families. The majority of them seemed to like the free and easy life they had chosen though.

One very young hobo among them was nicknamed
"Slippery" on account of his knack for eluding the
railroad guards. On more than one occasion, Slip-

pery had been nearly
"nabbed". He had
been whipped and
clubbed once and
bore the scars from that encounter. Daddy took
pity on him because he was so young and lonely;
and they became fast friends.

That night in camp, Daddy told Slippery about his
home and family. While the other hobos slept, Slippery was allowed to sample some of Betsy's rock-
candy, and he told Daddy how much he envied
him. To have a fine, warm home with a loving
family with his greatest goal in life, he said. That's
when Daddy invited Slippery home with him. He
knew full well Momma's feelings about hobos, but
he didn't care. If only for a little while, poor Slippery would sample home life.

They arose well before dawn the next morning.
It was best to board an empty box car under cover
of darkness. Slipperly talked excitedly about getting to meet our family and gingerly asked for
another taste of the rock-candy. Their ride would
end over twenty miles from where we lived, and
the balance of the journey would be made on foot.

The two men finally settled in to rest and to enjoy
the ride, huddled together for warmth. When the
train jerked suddenly to a stop, Daddy knew

something was amiss. He shook Slippery awake
and they cautiously peered out.

At one end of the long train, a railway inspector
and two guards stood talking. Their unexpected
search had already surprised two hobos, and one
lay heaped and beaten on the ground. As Daddy
watched, one of the guards kicked the limp form
of the hobo.

Without a word, Slippery leapt out of their box car
and motioned Daddy to follow him. Daddy hadn't
been involved in too many brushes with railroad
guards and was suddenly very glad for Slippery's
company. They slid beneath a boxcar, feeling certain they had not been spotted. On the other side
of the tracks lay a thick stand of woods and safety.

Slippery reached the thick undergrowth first and
lingered there for a moment.

"We gave 'em the slip, Stew" he whispered hoarse-
ly as Daddy joined him.

At that same moment, however, a guard appeared
from behind a bush. The man had obviously been
laying in wait, and he plucked Slippery off the
ground. Slippery dangled in the big man's grip and
then screamed in pan as the guard hit him with
his club.

With a furtive glance up the rails at two other guards who were fast approaching, Daddy turned back to help his friend.

"Get outta here, Stew!" Slippery screamed.

Daddy ignored that plea. Instead, he tackled the guard, knocking him off his feet. Dazed in his fall, the guard let loose his grip on Slippery, and he was able to join Daddy in flight. They hid in some thick briars near a pond and waited there until long after the train had pulled out.

Slippery limped a bit, but was otherwise all right. He felt Daddy had saved his life, being certain-sure those guards would have done him in. Daddy shook violently when he recalled their close call and vowed then never to take such a chance again. He would find a way to be closer to his family, eliminating the need to "hobo". They walked the rest of the way to our house, finally managing to arrive just before midnight on Betsy's birthday.

Momma was disgruntled about Daddy's unexpected guest, but she didn't dare complain. She simply woke Betsy, and then fixed the two men a hearty supper. It was a happy reunion with Daddy, even though Betsy did not fully wake until Daddy displayed what was left of the rock-candy.

Slippery spent the night in Momma's and Daddy's featherbed, even though Momma

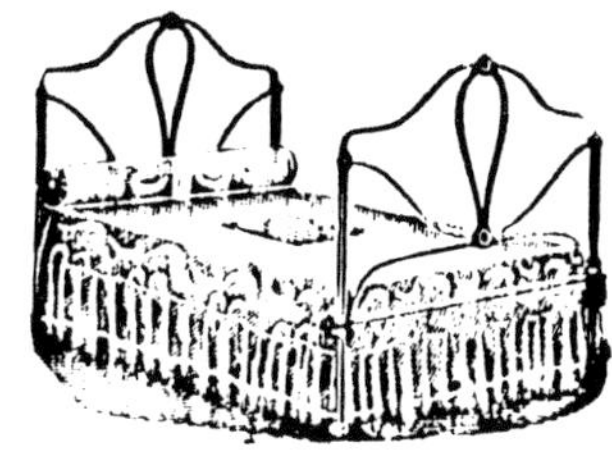

heartily disapproved. Daddy explained that Slippery had never slept in a real bed before, and he wanted to afford him that opportunity.

The next morning, Slippery lingered only long enough to sample Momma's breakfast. Then he was off to "ride the rails" again. He embraced Daddy before leaving, and I was sure his eyes became kind of teary.

We never saw Slippery again after that, even though Daddy gave him a standing invitation to visit. We sort of hoped, though, that Slippery had found an occupation less hazardous than hobo-ing . . . and that, perhaps, he had eventually settled down with a family of his own . . . and a nice feather bed.

CHAPTER XII

THAT CLUMSY REINDEER

hristmas, for my family, was not an occasion for extravagant gift-giving. Even Santa Claus seemed to have fallen on hard times. What we lacked in material possessions, however, we more than recouped in holiday cheer. One Christmas in particular was rather grim for us and a season when even the usual holiday

good spirits were lacking. Daddy's work as carpenter was seasonal, at best, and had played-out by autumn that year. On the advice of Uncle Ivan, who was also out of work, both men went southward in search of jobs. They were able to find work in a large factory and returned home jubilant.

To be closer to their new jobs, the men decided our families should move to a little town called Benbow. It was also decided that our families should live together and share expenses. Though neither Momma nor Aunt Julia relished the thought of having to move, they both recognized the need to do so. The prospect of spending a harsh Missouri winter without a man in the house was frightening.

Our belongings were stacked high in the back of Daddy's wagon. Our old horse was slow and plod-ding, and we worried that it might not make the long journey. Momma was heavy with child and was allowed to ride in the back of the wagon. The rest of us followed on foot.

We set out on a cold November morning during

(106)

a freezing drizzle. The chill seemed to cut through our clothing like a knife, and my feet quickly numbed. Every few miles, we had to stop to allow the younger children to rest. We older children had to carry the very small ones, and the going was quite slow. Somehow, Daddy's old horse found the strength, as did we, to reach Benbow just before sunset.

To me, Benbow did not seem inviting. I immediately missed the hills, hollers, and the lazy river of Hannibal. Benbow was on flat land; about as dull a place as I'd ever seen. Town folk peered at us through windows as we urged the horse down Benbow's barren streets. Now and then, stray dogs would nip at our heels or chase the wagon wheels. Though Daddy and Ivan talked enthusiastically about our "wonderful" new home, we were not cheered. So far, our welcome had been disappointing, at best.

For economic reasons, our lodgings were a grave disappointment, too. Our house was on the out-

skirts of town, bordered by a smelly little creek. It was a very small place, and the old clapboard siding was in dire need of repair. Many of the windows had been broken, and the front door had a huge hole in it.

One end of the house was being used for a corn-crib by the farmer who owned it, and Momma feared rats had taken the place over. Its interior was blanketed in dust and cobwebs, but Momma and Aunt Julia didn't complain. Instead, they immediately busied themselves at cleaning and organizing.

For lack of better accommodations, Daddy divided one of the tiny bedrooms with a blanket. Uncle Ivan's boys made sleeping pallets on one side of the blanket, while my sisters and I slept on the other. The men folk then toted in our few belongings and set to work patching holes in the house. The place was heated by one tiny stove, and it seemed to take an eternity to get the chill out.

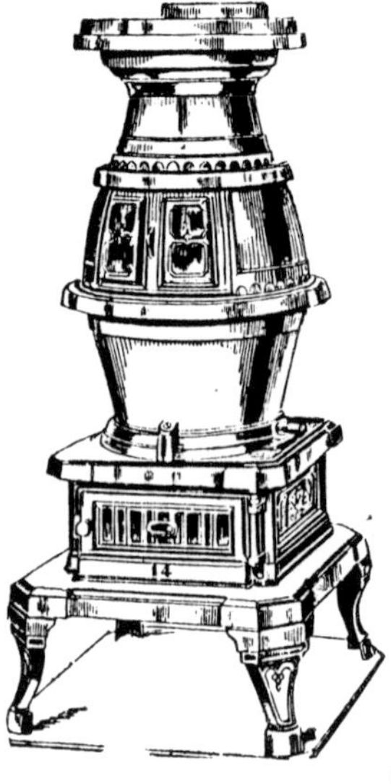

Late one night, Daddy and Ivan went hunting and managed to bring back several rabbits. We ate well the next day. Then Daddy showed us how to ice fish, carving a small hole in the ice of a pond near our house. At about the time my hands would turn completely numb from cold, someone would "spell" me awhile at our fishing hole. Though the fish we caught were small, they were a welcome change of pace from the wild game.

All in all, we had begun to settle into our

new home. Everyone looked forward to the time when Daddy and Ivan would bring home their earnings, and we even began to look forward to a proper Christmas celebration.

Then, only a few days before their scheduled start of work, Daddy's new foreman came to call. The man held his hat in his hands and looked sorrowful. He asked Daddy and Uncle Ivan outdoors to talk, and we sensed something was amiss. Daddy seldom raised his voice in anger, but he did on that day. He shouted at the man.

We found out that the plant Daddy and Ivan were scheduled to work in was being closed down. Both men sort of slumped over when they related the news to Momma and Aunt Julia, just like something had knocked the backbone right out of them. There was no recourse but to seek work elsewhere. Daddy seemed confident that jobs could be found in Peoria but he hesitated about traveling so far away. After all, my Momma was due to have a baby any time. Another long trip by wagon might prove hazardous for her and the baby.

After some deliberation, Momma urged Daddy and Ivan to go alone to Peoria. She bravely maintained that "Us wimmenfolk kin manage here jes fine".

On the day that Daddy and Uncle Ivan set out for Peoria, both Momma and Aunt Julia seemed cheer-

ful. But by the time the men had wound their way out of sight down our lane, both women were crying.

Our meager supply of groceries didn't last long. Daddy had built a few rabbit traps for us, but after the first snow, even the traps produced little. Pearl and I continued ice fishing until the pond became too frozen over to break through. We were finally reduced to one meal a day, and it was a mighty slim meal at that.

Finally, in desperation, Momma took to "borrowing" corn from the farmer's corn-crib. There weren't many tasty ways to fix the corn, but it kept us from starving.

Daddy and Uncle Ivan weren't able to find work
right away. They lived in "hobo camps", and we
didn't know until much later how close they came
to starving. In her letters to Daddy, Momma still
maintained a brave image. She had no desire to
worry our menfolk with our day-to-day stuggles.

December brought a thick blanket of snow to Benbow. Except for our daily excursions in search of
firewood, we were confined indoors. Daddy's old

horse keeled over early one wintry morning, and
we mourned his death. Miraculously, that night we
had fresh meat for supper. I suspected that
Momma had butchered our horse, but I didn't dare
mention my suspicions.

In mid-December, momma's baby was born. It was
premature and stillborn. Aunt Julia's boys prepared
a small grave in the frozen ground, and we all cried
a lot. It seemed all of Momma's worries and fears
came gushing forth as she read from her Bible over
the baby's grave. Momma, who had prayed
fervently for a healthy child and an end to our suffering, despaired.

(111)

In our day-to-day struggle for survival, however, there was little time for mourning. The Christmas holidays loomed nearer, and we children were cheered by the prospect of Daddy's return home. Momma did not want to burden us with the fact that our father and Uncle Ivan would not be home for Christmas. They had finally found work in Peoria, they wrote, but they would have to stay on their jobs through the holidays. Momma encouraged our belief that Santa Claus would pay his yearly visit, even though he would probably bring "slim pickins'".

Aunt Julia and Momma had carefully hoarded away popcorn for the holidays. We popped enough for tree-decorating, and then hungrily devoured the rest.

A small, scrawny cedar tree was erected in our living room, and adorned with strings of popcorn. Though devoid of other ornaments, the tree was a pretty reminder of the joyful season. At its base Momma carefully arranged the creche. The tiny Nativity figures had been hand-carved by Daddy, and Momma got a far-away look in her eyes as she held them.

Before tucking us in that night, Momma reminded us once again not to expect too much of old Santie Claus.

"Been a mean year for ever'one," she said. "But

I reckon he'll come anyways." We slept then,
secure in the knowledge that we would awake to
find "treats" beneath our Christmas tree.

Somehow, during the night, stray dogs were en-
ticed by the smell of the fresh popcorn. Those dogs
managed to break through the patched front door,
and they laid waste to our Christmas tree, devour-
ing every bit of the home-made ornamentation.
We woke up the next morning to find the room

in complete disarray, and the little cedar tree laying on its side. Amazingly, the tiny Nativity figures
had withstood the onslaught. They remained
perfectly in place, just as Momma had arranged
them.

Momma's excuse for the upheaval was a flash of
brilliance.

"Them derned clumsy reindeer! Shore wish old
Santie woulda tied 'em up outside, steada lettin'
'em in to kick our tree over."

Though the younger kids believed her story, I began to have my doubts about Santa.

We stared dejectedly at what was left of our Christmas tree, noticing with some concern that there were no gifts beneath it. Momma had slipped off to her room and returned carrying many small packages. Each was neatly wrapped in brown paper, and tied with yarn.

"I suppose Old Santie figured these would be safer over in my room."

She handed a package to each of us, and then smiled as we opened them. I immediately recognized the handiwork as Momma's, not Santa's. She had painstakingly knitted a new pair of winter-socks for each of us.

Our Christmas cheer thus revived, we spent the day singing hymns and carols, and laughing a bit over the antics of Santa's reindeer. To complete our celebration, Daddy and Uncle Ivan came home late that evening. They brought a fresh supply of groceries, and we all gorged ourselves. Though he could ill afford it, Daddy had even squandered a bit of money on fresh oranges and peppermint sticks. Our holiday was complete and happy.

CHAPTER XIII

THE SOUP-KITCHEN
AND
RELIEF SWEATERS

he old saying "Poor, but Proud" applied to my family. Though we were sometimes desperate for food and clothing, my parents found it difficult to accept charity. Most of the time, we managed to get by, but I recall a time when my Daddy had to put his pride aside.

We had just returned to Hannibal after Daddy's bout with malaria, and he was not fully recovered. He thought he was well enough to resume work for the railroad but found his job was not waiting

for him. As with most of the other folks we knew, Daddy was out of work and desperate. I suppose his thin and gaunt form didn't present a too-promising employee, for he was repeatedly turned away. He searched for odd jobs door to door, hoping we could subsist on his meager earnings.

Momma took in wash and began sewing to help out. Gracie found work at a local factory, even though she had to lie about her age to get the job. To reduce the number of mouths Daddy had to

feed, Selma moved in with a girlfriend. Pearl and I collected and sold rags, but the pickings were slim. It seemed every other kid in town had the same notion.

We were miserably hungry most of the time. My folks did without so that we could have an extra morsel of food, but there was never enough. Momma would not allow complaints, admonishing us to be thankful for what little we had. She had

a knack of always knowing someone worse off
than we, although at times, I sincerely doubted
that.

On those summer evenings, Daddy always had the
company of neighborhood men. They would congregate on our porch or in the yard to share their

miseries and woes. Most of them, like Daddy, were
in dire straits, and all lived in fear of being sent
to the poor-house.

Then one evening, one of Daddy's friends mentioned the "Soup Kitchen". He called the place a
godsend, and described how the free food had saved his family on more than one occasion. The mention of free food immediately caught our attention.
As usual that evening, we had left the supper table
still hungry. The man didn't describe the Soup Kitchen as charity, a fact Daddy found quite in-
teresting, because it was commonly used by the
folks in our neighborhood. Folks were required to

"sign up" before getting their free food and to bring a clean empty bucket. The man described the thick, hearty, bean soup, and our mouths began to water.

That evening, my folks talk- ed in hushed whispers, and I knew Momma was "work- ing on" Daddy to allow us to visit the Soup Kitchen. I hoped that Daddy's pride wouldn't override common sense and dreamed of delicious and filling soup that night.

My hopes came true. By morning, I suppose Momma had worn Daddy down. Right after we got up, Dad- dy instructed us to go the Soup Kitchen that after- noon. For a change, we would have a hearty and filling supper . . . charity or no.

Pearl and I were each given a clean lard bucket and set off on foot for the Lindell Avenue Soup Kitchen. The delicious aroma of bean soup greeted us from over a block away, and we broke into a dead run.

People lined the length of the block, and we took our position at the end of that line. I began to worry that, with so many people there to feed, the Soup Kitchen might run out before filling our buckets. It seemed to take an eternity to move forward in that long line, and my resentment of the other people there grew with each passing second. Pearl shared my resentment. She began to talk about the good soup the kitchen offered and then loudly proclaimed that it hadn't made her sick in almost two days.

Folks ahead of us in line turned to listen, as Pearl went on to describe the terrible food poisoning she had suffered. Recognizing Pearl's intent, I stifled a giggle and interrupted her.

"The food poisoning ain't so bad," I told her loudly. "It's them derned cockroaches that makes me sick."

Folks began to leave the line ahead of us, and the ones who remained were abuzz with whispers.

As the Soup Kitchen line quickly thinned, we found ourselves nearing the front. I'm not sure what I expected the Soup Kitchen to be like, but what greeted me was rather disappointing. I  resembled a small trolley-car, with windows lining its sides. A table had been set up outside the trolley, and people sat there looking up names and writing in a book.

When it came our turn, a kindly lady asked my name and address, and I told her eagerly. All the while, I tried to stifle my growling stomach. When Pearl was interrogated by the lady in the same manner, her responses shocked me. She listed her real name, even though she had always used my Daddy's name. For her address, she listed the house across the street from ours. The lady didn't question what, to me, was an obvious lie. Pearl later explained that only one bucket of food was allowed per household, and our large family would require both of our buckets full. I had to admire Pearl's quick thinking.

Our family ate well that night, relishing every morsel of the delicious broth. Even Daddy had to

allow that the soup was delicious and that accepting it wasn't all that bad. Thereafter, we made frequent trips to the Soup Kitchen.

Having swallowed his pride in one regard, Daddy found it a little easier to consider other "charities". When he heard about the free relief sweaters being offered to children, Daddy eagerly accepted it. He took us to the Relief Office downtown, and we were each measured for fit. I was real proud with the brand new brick-red heavy knit sweater 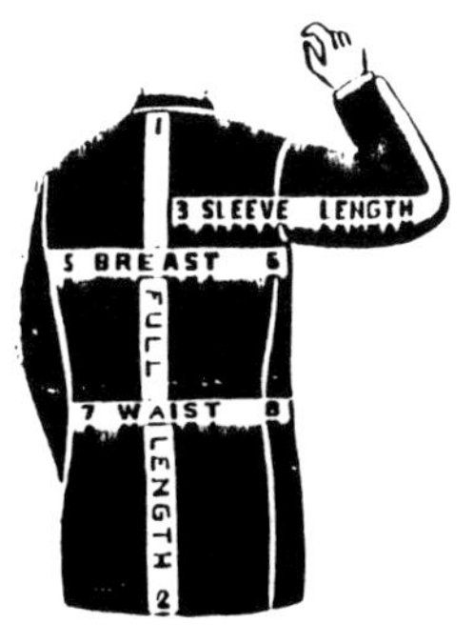 issued to me. It was the first new item of apparel I'd ever worn, and I couldn't wait to show it off at school the next day.

I realized the next day that over half the kids in town were in possession of the same type of sweater. Those of us wearing the "relief-sweaters" gathered in a large group on the playground, meekly trying to ignore the teasing and taunting of the other children. Those thick, red sweaters were the surest sign of poverty, and I was suddenly very ashamed of mine. I returned from school that evening with the sweater stuffed roughly into my lunch-bucket.

 Momma was naturally curious about my change of heart, and I poured out my story.

"Relief sweaters ain't no good!" I cried. "They jus' mean you is poor . . . poor as dirt."

I insisted I would never wear the red sweater again, and Momma didn't argue with me. She seemed sympathetic, in fact. I was sent to bed that evening and told not to worry.

"Things will look much better by morning."

(121)

Momma stayed up all night, and we found her dozing in a living room chair the next morning. In her lap was my relief sweater, except that it had been drastically altered. With painstaking care, Momma had embroidered tiny hearts and flowers in varying colors all over the sweater. I gazed at it in awe, unable to believe the transformation. It was the most beautiful sweater I had ever seen.

I wore it proudly to school that day, secure in the knowledge that my sweater was "one of a kind". The "ohs" and "ahs" of my classmates confirmed the beauty of the sweater. It was no longer a symbol of poverty. It was my Momma's very unique creation . . . and a symbol of her love for me.

CHAPTER XIV

THE "DAY OF RECKONING"

n the nineteen thirties, folks had little knowledge of comets, meteors and the like. Being in the middle of the "Bible Belt, however, meant that we were well aware of the Scriptures regarding "Armageddon". According to the Good Book, Armageddon seemed very real and very close at hand. Newspapers and the radio carried accounts of a huge fire ball approaching from Heaven. Many predicted when and

where it would strike. Everyone most certainly agreed that the fireball was headed towards the Midwest . . . and that it most certainly spelled doom for Hannibal.

The more religious folks among us interpreted that fire ball as God's final wrath, and they preached repentance all the more. Our sleepy little town that usually seemed unaffected by current events was thrown into an immediate panic.

Even my folks were shaken. Momma insisted the Bible prophesies had come true. Daddy insisted that we, like the rest of town, find a place to hide. Everyone around  Hannibal knows there are more caves then you can shake a stick at. Most of the townspeople had retreated to the larger, more comfortable caves on the south side. Daddy, however, knew of a smaller cave over near Oakwood, and that's where he wanted to take us.

Momma vehemently refused to go with us. She insisted that, if God was choosing to destroy the world, there was no safe haven to be found anywhere. She remained at home, along with a few of her women-friends, and they formed prayer sessions. The rest of us accompanied Daddy to the Oakwood cave. We had two #2 washtubs filled with supplies drawn from our meager pantry and a little clothing. We made the trek on foot.

As we walked down the road, our usually busy streets seemed abandoned. It was an eerie feeling, seeing all the empty houses and stores. Now and then, a stray dog would bark or whine at us, but there seemed to be no life at all.

The cave Daddy
directed us to was
dark and musty. As
we busied ourselves
making sleeping
pallets on the floor
and unpacking, Daddy
constructed a
makeshift barricade
for the cave opening.

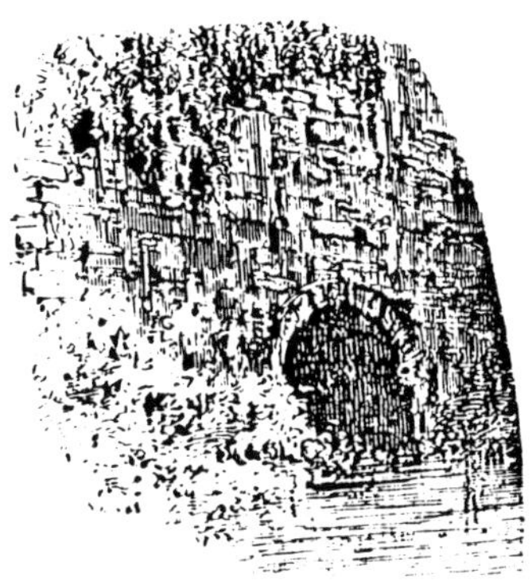

Then we settled in to await the "siege". For my sisters and me, living in that cave spelled adventure. The excitement of it soon wore off, though, for we were not allowed to venture out for several days. Daddy, on the other hand, made the journey back home to check on Momma every day. We had grown quite tired of the confinement and of the steady diet of canned beans and raw 'taters. Every day Daddy would bring back fresh accounts of the fire ball. The newspapers were assured it was headed straight for Hannibal, even though they played down the part of it destroying the town.

Then, only four days after we had gone to live in the cave, the great fire ball arrived. We could see its fiery trail in the night sky late one evening, and afterward Daddy placed the barricade across the opening. None of us slept that night, full of fear and apprehension after our "sighting". The next morning, along about sun-up, we heard a sound like a faraway thunderclap.

I even imagined I felt the earth shaking beneath

us, and my little sisters began to cry hysterically.

Daddy somehow managed to calm everyone down, and then gingerly peeked out through his barricade. The bright sun shone in, and our world looked much the same as it had the day before. There were no flames, as we had been told to expect, no charred and scorched earth. Quickly, we packed up our pallets and set out for home.

The city streets were crowded with other folks, too, and every one seemed extremely relieved that the fire ball had not wrecked the havoc forecasted. At home Momma had prepared a huge meal for us, and we all ate hungrily.

Afterward, a friend of Daddy's stopped by to tell him he had actually seen the place where the fireball hit. It was in a small, open pasture near the edge of town, and he told us practically everyone in town had turned out to view it. We naturally had to satisfy our curiosity about the thing so we agreed to accompany the man.

The fireball, or meteor, had left a huge crater in the ground. A crowd had formed around that charred pit, and people talked animatedly. When we had finally managed to wriggle to the front and were able to peek into the hole, I was surprised.

I'm not sure what I had expected to find, but the huge rock that confronted me was a disappointment. My family and I had spent a miserable and interminable amount of time in a dark old cave . . . all for nothing.

For several weeks after that, newspapers carried reports of Hannibal's fallen meteor, and everyone began to laugh at the panic and fear the town had been put through. Some folks continued to insist that Armageddon was at hand, but they were ignored. Folks resumed their usual sinful lives, with a come-what-may attitude.

The meteor became something of a tourist attraction, until it was finally dug up and hauled away so the field could be tilled. Hannibal was never bothered by fire balls from Heaven again.

CHAPTER XV

A CHILD OUT OF WEDLOCK

ince I never took much interest in household chores, Momma often humored me by allowing me to work outside. That's why, on that sunny Saturday morning, when she asked me to clean her room, I winced with pain. Momma saw my look with those "eyes in the back of her head" from clear across the room. I was then dispatched to the unwanted chore with a sore behind.

In spite of my lack of motivation, however, the work wasn't all that bad. In my parent's room was a treasure-trove of secret and untouchable things . . . like the kewpie-doll in Momma's trunk, or the faded diary she carefully hid beneath her bed. I never took anything, but I got sheer delight out of knowing I had uncovered the treasures.

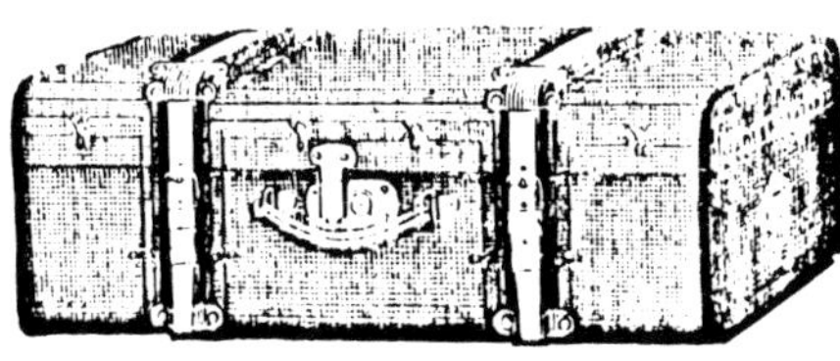

I wasn't prepared for the surprise I found that day, however. While polishing the picture frames on Momma's wall, I discovered a neatly printed little

document I had never noticed before. It was my parents' marriage license, and I was relieved to know that that document existed. I'd had my doubts about the validity of their marriage since the time we discovered some of our neighbors were "living in sin". I read the faded certificate happily and then noticed a very disturbing fact. The date on the document was only a few years back. At the time, I would have been almost two years old, and my sister, Lily, about nine months.

I had heard about "illegitimate" children on many occasions. Momma's gossip with Aunt Beth had been enlightening in that regard, and I was well-versed in the matter. The thought had never struck me that I just might be illegitimate. I raced from Momma's room with tear-filled eyes.

Lily stopped me on the way to the privy, though she knew I was in no mood to be pestered. She ignored my tears and angry expression and began to whine and complain. When I couldn't get rid of her with the usual slap or pinch, I became infuriated.

"Bastard!" I shouted at her. "You are just a stupid

little bastard! You and me is BOTH bastards!"

Lily was familiar enough with cuss-words to recognize my foul language. She made straightway to tell Momma about it, as was her usual habit. For once I didn't care.

Instead of the usual "mouth-soaping" Momma handed down for cussing, she surprised me by remaining calm. She took me aside, and I noticed the very sad expression on her face.

Momma was never one to mince words. She sighed heavily, and then tried to explain why I shouldn't call myself and my sisters that.

"Lonie-girl", she whispered, "You got to believe me, now child . . . you and Lily wasn't borned out of wedlock and that is the Gospel Truth."

I nodded, more to reassure her. My curiosity about the matter had definitely not been satisfied. She admonished me never to speak of the matter again, but I needed more information.

That night when Daddy came home, I broached the subject with him. He was a very understanding sort, being able to recall his own childhood so vividly and all, so he took great care to explain things well.

I was shocked to discover that my Momma had been married to someone before Daddy. It shocked me even more to learn that my three older sisters were really half sisters.

(131)

In Momma's younger days, she was quite a beauty. She had little trouble attracting suitors, but Grandma and Poppa Scheckhorst insisted on arranging on a match for her.

When Okie Tankster came to call, they immediately decided he was "right" for Momma. They encouraged a quick courtship, and Momma married Okie when she was only thirteen.

Momma didn't argue with the match, for Okie was quite handsome even though he was over nine years older than she. He had a nice profitable farm over at Shelbina, and she figured he would take good care of her.

Momma quickly bore him two daughters . . . my sisters, Selma and Gracie. When she bore him a son, Okie told her he was well satisfied with the size of their family. Momma became pregnant (with my sister Pearl) again, and that's when Okie up and left.

Abandoned on that isolated farm with three young babies, Momma became frightened and lonely. When her baby boy suddenly took sick, she was at her wit's end. She decided to return to live with Grandma and Poppa. Shortly after that, the baby died of pneumonia.

It was a heavy burden for Grandma to keep the

girls with her. At the time, several of my aunts and uncles were still living at home, and Grandma began to wonder how she would feed everyone. She finally arranged for Momma to take a job at the hotel where she worked as a cook. Momma's wages would be completely turned over to Grandma every week to help cover the expense of room and board.

Then, one night at the hotel, Grandma caught one of the male guests getting fresh with Momma. The man was drunk and insisted on dragging my pretty mother back to his room with him. Grandma went after him with a wet-mop, beating the man almost senseless. That's when she decided Momma had better quit working.

Though Grandma constantly nagged Momma to "get out and find another man", most folks thought that would be a futile effort. After all, who would possibly want a woman - no matter how pretty - with three young children in tow? Momma despaired of ever marrying again and sort of resigned herself to a single life. She resigned herself, also, to the fact that Grandma would never give her any peace about it.

When Aunt Tillie brought her new boyfriend home to meet the family, he took an instant liking to Momma. Aunt Tillie was a little hurt when he indicated his

interest in her sister, so she proceeded to tell him how Momma was married and had three kids. Remarks like that had sent many a young suitor scurrying. This fellow, however, didn't seem to mind.

Because of their desperation to marry Momma off, the young man passed Grandma's and Poppa's scrutiny easily. Momma, however, didn't take much of an interest in the man. He wasn't nearly as good looking as Okie had been, and not nearly as serious either. The fellow liked nothing better than a sip of corn likker and a good laugh. Then there was the fact that he was a "collegeman", having spent a few years at the agricultural school over in Springfield. Momma must have been quite intimidated by that, for she had only a third-grade education.

The young suitor was my Daddy, and in time, he pursuaded Momma to marry him. By that time, Okie Tankster had been gone for a few years, and everyone figured him dead. Grandma fetched the Preacher-Man home one night, and saw to it that Momma and Daddy were married proper-like.

They moved to a small furnished apartment in Hannibal, and I was born a year later. From the start, I was Daddy's "little Lonie-girl". It's not that he loved me any more than my sisters, but just that I was his first. I favored Momma, having the blue-grey eyes Daddy admired so much, and he doted on me.

I was only six months old when Okie Tankster showed up on our doorstep.

Momma nearly fainted when she saw him there, but she invited him in. Okie laughed aloud when she remarked at how he looked mighty healthy for a "dead man".

He seemed real pleased that his daughters were being well cared for and politely inquired if Momma was happy with her new "husband". He went on to tell her how she was living in sin; and

Momma began to cry. She explained how she had grown to love my Daddy dearly, and how she didn't think she could live without him.

Okie just had to stick around and meet the man Momma raved about. He was careful to point out to Daddy, on his arrival home from work, that the wedding license hanging on their wall was a worthless piece of paper.

Daddy was a lot disgruntled about Okie's showing up so suddenly but listened politely as Okie rambled on. Okie's plan was to retrieve his three daughters and return with them to the farm in Shelbina.

He figured Daddy would be relieved to be rid of them and was taken aback when Daddy hollered "NO!"

Daddy then took great care to explain to Okie about how much he loved the three little girls; how they were like his own, and how they believed him to be their true father.

Daddy punctuated his remarks with a clenched fist very near Okie's nose, promising to do him harm if he didn't leave our little family alone.

He allowed that Okie had every right to see his kids and told him he wouldn't mind occasional

visits. Okie seemed satisfied with that arrangement
. . . but there was still the problem of Momma still
being legally wed to him. It was decided that, as
soon as Daddy could raise the money, a divorce
would be obtained.

Okie left that night, and returned only once to visit
his children. We later learned he had moved back
to Shelbina to farm. It took over a year for Daddy
to scrape up enough money for the divorce. But
about that time Selma took gravely ill. All of
Daddy's savings went toward her treatment, and
the divorce matter was postponed.

Finally after the birth of my sister, Lily, Daddy
figured the divorce was imperative. He took an extra job to earn more money and finally managed
to acquire enough. In the course of getting the
divorce paperwork completed, however, Daddy's
attorney found out that Okie Trankster had died
of pneumonia that winter.

Momma and Daddy had a private wedding ceremony at a downtown chapel. The license from that wedding was the one I had seen on Momma's wall, and it was her most prized possession.

Daddy finished his explanation with a hug. Then he whispered, soft and sweetly in my ear.

"Lonie-girl; you are just as legitimate as a child could ever be . . . and the beautiful proof of my love for your Momma. Let's not speak of this matter again."

Though Daddy's been gone over thirty years now, I can still recall his jubilant laughter that day, when Lily walked into the room and asked, "Daddy, . . . why'd Lee-Onie call me a badturd?"

CHAPTER XVI

ANGIE DOLL

hroughout my growing-up years, my family lived, from time to time, in a part of Hannibal called "The Bottoms". The term didn't make reference to the quality of land we lived on but only identified that area as the poorest section of Hannibal. Only two blocks away from us, and separated by the railroad tracks,

were more affluent neighbors. The railway formed a barricade that children of my district could not cross unless invited.

I was fortunate to have a glimpse of that "rich" side of town. I was invited to the area by my schoolteacher, who told me I would be hired to

tutor a young, sickly girl there.

The notion of being paid for something I enjoyed pleased me, so I accepted the job offer eagerly. I proudly announced to Momma and Daddy that night that I would soon be able to pay "room and board", as older sisters did.

I was in awe of the huge, fine house my teacher sent me to. A uniformed servant greeted me at the door, and I became suddenly self-conscious about the "everyday" clothes I wore. When Angie's

mother introduced herself, however, she seemed to take little notice of my appearance. Instead, she flashed a warm and welcoming smile, and I felt immediately comfortable in her presence.

Angie resided in a luxurious room upstairs, full of every type of toy imaginable. On my first visit to her, I spent most of our time together staring at her collection of dolls. I had never seen so many dolls in one place before; a fact Angie found quite humorous.

Weak and wane,
Angie seldom left
her bed. She was
propped up by a
mountain of
pillows and look-
ed all the more
tiny and helpless.
No one bothered
to explain Angie's
illness to me, so I
took it for
granted she
would one day
recover.

Only one year younger than I, she wasn't much
bigger than my baby brother. I could easily carry
her from the bed
to a big and or-
nate window in
her room. We
would sit at that
window, Angie
cradled in my
lap, and dream
about the "out-
side" world. That

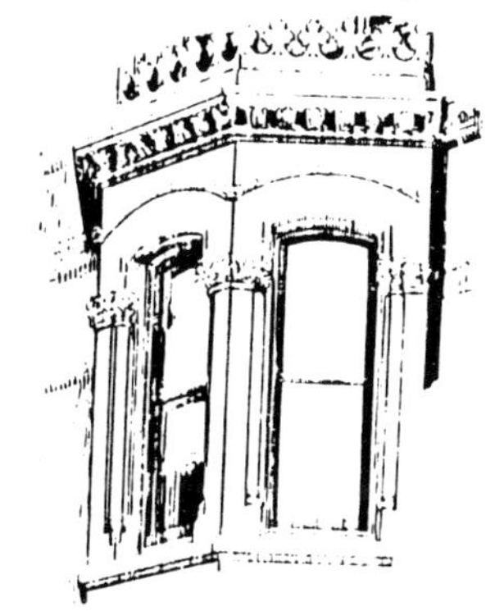

was a place Angie had not been allowed to know,
and she wanted more than anything to leave the
confines of her room to explore it.

Though intelligent and attentive, she took little interest in my tutoring. Instead, she would implore
me to tell stories or recite poetry I had composed.

(141)

Such a willing audience thrilled me, and I quickly complied. Oftentimes, we would set our books aside and settle down to "play". Angie's parents did not seem to mind our poor study-habits, and even seemed happy that I enjoyed playing with her.

I took particular delight in the two tiny twin dolls that were Angie's favorite toys. They were made of china, with perfect details, eyes that opened and closed, and corn-silk hair. One had brown eyes, and the other had blue eyes. Other than that, the dolls were alike in every detail. We could play with those dolls for hours on end, or at least until Angie grew too tired.

"Leona", she would whisper weakly; "I think the babies need a nap."

That was my cue to replace the dolls in their cradle and leave, so Angie could rest. Many times, I lingered at Angie's bedside until she had fallen asleep.

After many months of visiting Angie, I became
more puzzled about her condition. The recovery
I had expected wasn't happening; in fact, she seemed to grow worse with each passing day. I confronted her parents with my worries one evening.
I was told they didn't want to burden me with their
concerns, and that Angie would be just fine before
too long. I noticed the sadness in their voices and
could detect the tears they tried to stifle. I wanted
desperately to believe that Angie would be well
one day, but the nagging suspicion that something
was terribly wrong remained. Because of my being worried, I spent even more time with her,
bringing what cheer and happiness into her life I
could.

I guess it didn't sur-
prise me when
Angie's mother
came to call. I in-
stinctively knew
that Angie had died
during the night for
I hadn't gotten a
moment's rest. Still,
it was hard to face
the awful reality of her death. I continued my daily
treks to Angie's house, staring at her bedroom window longingly and recalling the many happy hours
spent with her. I would linger at the fancy iron
fence that surrounded her yard and imagine Angie
playing happily in the grass.

One day I watched with great sorrow as boxes and
trunks of Angie's belongings were carried from the

house. Angie's mother directed her servants to dispose of the items, and I began to cry. I suppose she heard my sobbing, because the next thing I knew she was patting my head tenderly. I could tell she had been crying, too, and I felt very sorry

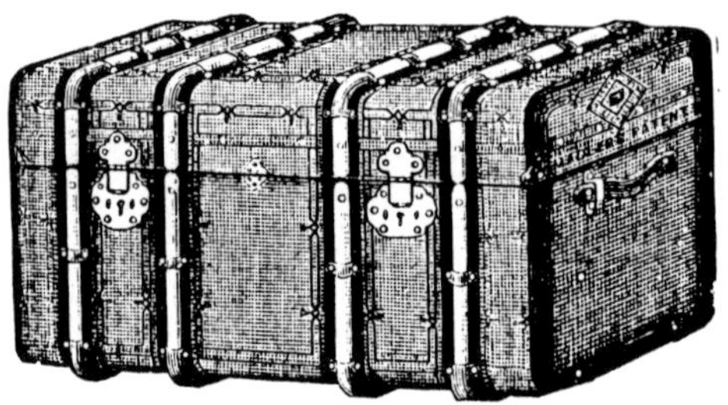

for her. We sat on the porch step, silent and pensive for a long while. Then, she took my hand and led me to the stack of trunks.

"There is something here, Leona, that I think Angie wanted you to have."

When she took those two twin dolls out of a trunk, I accepted them eagerly. I cried all the more at her generosity and thanked her with a hug. She seemed quite overcome, for she dabbed at her fresh tears.

"You take good care of her babies. They were her favorites, you know."

I nodded and hugged the dolls tightly to me.

Momma insisted that I share the dolls with Lily, though I much protested. Finally, I relented and gave her the blue-eyed one. Lily quickly broke it, and then tried to take possession of the remain-

ing one. It was my most-prized possession,
however, and I wouldn't even allow her to touch
it. I treated the doll as if it were a real child . . .
and named it "Angie".

CHAPTER XVII

HOW'D MOMMA KNOW?

I n my day, a child's neighborhood encompassed the whole town. We were free to roam and explore to our heart's content, and Momma never seemed to fret or worry for our safety. Shortly after sunrise during the summer months, we would disappear. I don't think Momma ever had a clue as to where we went or what we did . . . except for one occasion when she managed to locate me.

A light fog settled over our little valley-town during the hottest days of summer. Daddy called such fogs the "Summer-time Haze". He said they were caused by all the heat and humidity that was trapped between the hills around town. The haze was usually burned away by about noon by the hot summer sun.

While the haze still shrouded our sleeping village, I liked to climb the highest peek in town and survey the place. My vantage spot had been referred to as "Lover's Leap", and I thought it was quite special.

The Leap consisted of a flat rock that extended from a hillside; one of the highest hills in town, in fact. From that point, I could look out across

the farms to one side where I could see the Mississippi as it snaked its way northward towards Quincy. Or I could look out across Hannibal. It was an especially beautiful sight when the haze began to lift, and it fired my already active imagination.

In one instant, I was transformed into a fairy princess, overseeing my "cloudvillage" far below. At other times, I was a beautiful opera-star fairly bursting my lungs for the cheering crowds below me. I sang so loudly that some of the neighborhood hounds

(148)

would join in. I prided myself on the fact that I
could out-howl any of them.

In our large family, clothing 
was scarce. My summertime
wardrobe consisted of a few
handsewn chemises, not
much more than camisoles
with plain skirts. That summer, however, Momma had
salvaged a bright red scrap
of material, and she used it
to fashion my dresses. The
red apparel was "pretty on me", Momma said, so
I never missed an opportunity to wear it.

Early that summer morning, I climbed to the Leap,
being very careful not to soil my red dress. I felt
particularly attractive that day and began my
operatic aria almost before reaching the summit.

I had fashioned a dandeloin "tiara" and necklace.
The problem with dandeloin jewelry is the pesky
ants that come out of it. At any rate, that day even
the ants didn't bother me. I skipped out to the Leap
happily and sat on its very edge, dangling my legs
over the side.

I was on top of the world; master of all I surveyed,
and thrilled to be alive. Though I could see my
whole town quite clearly, I felt certain my town
couldn't see me. Far below me, vehicles looked
like tiny toys, and people reminded me of the ants
I had been pestered with.

As was my usual habit, I glanced in the area of
my house. I finally recognized Momma's heavily-
laden clothes line in our backyard and could see

the figures of my mother and sister moving about.
Laundry was my least favorite chore, and I con-
gratulated myself on the fact that, once more, I
had safely eluded it.

Our clothes had to be boiled in a big tub in the
yard. Then, after my fingers had been singed raw
by the hot fabrics, I was forced to "wring" them
nearly dry. I had never acquired a talent for wringing clothes to Momma's satisfaction . . . a fact she
was always too eager to point out. I had even had
bad dreams in which I grew to be an old lady doing nothing but laundry in a big old tub.

But today, I sure wasn't an old lady doing laundry in a big tub and I was enjoying my perch on The Leap.

I watched with some amusement as my sister, Selma, did the chore. Selma was a "natural born wringer", and I envied her that ability. The chubby figure of Momma moved slowly about the yard, hanging clothes on the line and stopping now and then to mop her brow. Momma did not know of my penchant for dangerous heights, and I felt secure in the knowledge that she never would.

I remained on my perch and continued spying for quite some time. Then my growling tummy reminded me I had had no breakfast. Though I tried to stifle the hunger pains, it was no use; I would have to feed myself. It occurred to me that it might now be safe to return home, since Selma had assumed the unwanted chores. I skipped down the steep hill and to the shortcut that led to my backyard.

I had only barely entered the yard, when Momma's chubby hand smartly boxed my ears. Surprised, I stumbled and fell. Momma clubbed me again, though I tried to get away. I despised whippings anyway, but a whipping for no apparent reason was absolutely unbearable . . . and I told her so.

That's when Momma proceeded to tell me - very loudly and at great length-why I was being whipped.

"If'n I ever catch you . . .", she shouted angrily; "Up on that there cliff again, young lady; I will KILL YOU DEAD." Her words were punctuated with those flailing fists, and I knew full well she would have no qualms about "doing away" with her youngin. I swore to her that I would never climb to The Leap again. Course, I had my fingers a bit crossed at the time.

Selma told me my bright, red dress had been a dead giveaway for Momma. I guess the sight of me, sitting on the very tip of The Leap with my legs dangling down gave Momma a real start. It didn't help matters much when Selma told her I visited the spot just about every day.

I continued my daily climbs to The Leap, but I was a bit sneaky about it after that. I also became very discreet about my bright apparel after that incident, too.

CHAPTER XVIII

RAG PICKERS

nterprising young people of my day had many ways to make money, providing they didn't mind long hours and strenuous labor. I worked in the fields, shucking corn, hauling hay, picking apples, and the like. But by far, my most profitable venture was "rag-pickin".

Rags were plentiful if you knew where to look for them. There was a ready market, too, though I often wondered why Roth's Salvage seemed anxious to buy my rags. I made the many dumps and junkyards around town regular stops on my daily sojourns, and could easily fill two or three sacks of rags a week. The rags had to be laundered before selling and then packed into the back of my wagon. After I had accumulated a week's worth of pickings, it was time for the trip to Roth's. At that time, the journey was about ten miles from the house in the "Bottoms".

I suppose some kids had cheated Roth's at one time or another, because they had a habit of splitting open the rag-sacks — just to be sure I hadn't thrown in a few rocks. Then the rags would be carefully weighed. Often, my week's work only netted me a few pennies, but that was adequate for my needs. I would rush off to spend my wages on ice cream, penny-candy, and writing paper.

One year, though, I decided to do something special for my Momma. Mother's Day was fast approaching, and I wanted to surprise her with a gift. In our family, gift-giving was unusual. We usually

celebrated special occasions with Momma's home made fritters or cookies, and that seemed adequate. But that particular Mother's Day seemed extra special to me and I wanted to show Momma how much I loved her.

When I confided my plans to Lily, she insisted on
helping. Though Lily was not fond of hard work,
I must admit she did her share. Together, we rose
at dawn every morning to begin our day of rag
pickin'.

Often the stench of those junkyards lingered with
us after we had returned home, and I knew
Momma was suspicious. I don't know how Lily
managed to keep our secret, because she had a
remarkabale knack for "spilling the beans". Our
neighbor lady, Mrs. Gentry, knew of the plan for
Momma's gift and offered to help us. We used her
wash-tub to clean our rags, and then hung them
over her fence to dry. When Momma noticed the
rags hanging there, she naturally assumed Mrs.
Gentry had started rag-pickin', figuring the old
woman had fallen on hard times. We allowed her
to believe that, and even helped her carry in food
to our good neighbor.

We couldn't tell
Momma the truth,
of course. She
would have in-
sisted upon using
our rag money
for groceries. The
money had to be
carefully hidden
each day, and we

found a perfect spot for it. High above our porch
and atop one of the white pillars, I found a small
hole. It had ample room for our savings after I had
cleared out the birds' nest. It became our secret

bank. Lily, who felt quite certain bandits and owl-
hoots might rob us, kept a nightly vigil over our
hidden money.

The day before Mother's Day, we finally retriev-
ed our loot and counted it. We had managed to
save quite a bit. I thought, though, that Lily was
a bit disappointed. She figured our hard labor
would surely have netted more of a "fortune" than
the stack of coins we had. We set out, however,
for Hannibal's downtown and the big Mercantile
store.

I agonized over the gift selections. Momma was
far too practical for perfume or jewelry, and the

clerks suggestion of
lingerie made me
giggle. Somehow, I
couldn't picture my
too-plump Momma
in those lacy un-
dies. Then I recall-
ed the fresh "leak"
that had developed
in Momma's old
washtub, and decided to buy her a new one. There
was just enough money leftover for a pair of white
stockings, which I knew Momma need badly. She
had been wearing my Daddy's old cast off socks,
and they struck her well above the knees.

That following Sunday, Lily and I were bursting
with anticipation. Somehow, we managed to pa-
tiently sit by and wait while our sisters presented
Momma with their homemade Mother's Day cards.

Then we snuck over to Mrs. Gentry's to fetch our gifts. Mrs. Gentry just had to accompany us back home. She wanted to see Momma's reaction.

"Yer Momma's jus' gonna leap fer joy," she whispered as we walked in our back door.

Momma's reaction was grave disappointment. On seeing us toting in that new tub and socks, she began to cry. She bawled so hard, I began to get nervous.

I figured she must be mad as blazes about our having hidden the rag-money. I knew for sure we were in for a whipping.

At just about the time I had inched towards the door, Momma leaped toward me. She did the most unexpected thing. She hugged both Lily and me to her so hard we could hardly breathe.

"This is jes' the best . . . the most wonderful Mother's Day," she whispered. "And I'll never fergit it . . . ever!"

(157)

EPILOGUE

I hope you enjoyed this glimpse into a child's life in the 1930s.

I hope you've developed some of the love and affection for Momma, "Slippery", Mabel Brown, and all the rest of the other po' folk of those days.

God Bless You!

"Lonie-girl"

Need A Gift?

For

- **Shower** • **Birthday** • **Mother's Day** •
- **Anniversary** • **Christmas** •

Turn Page for Order Form
(Order Now While Supply Lasts!)

To Order Copies Of

MISSISSIPPI RIVER PO' FOLK

Please send me _______ copies of **Mississippi River Po' Folk** at $9.95 each. (Make checks payable to **QUIXOTE PRESS.**)

Name _______________________________________

Street _______________________________________

City _________________ State _______ Zip _______

Send Orders To:
Quixote Press
R.R. #4, Box 33B • Blvd. Station
Sioux City, Iowa 51109

- -

To Order Copies Of

MISSISSIPPI RIVER PO' FOLK

Please send me _______ copies of **Mississippi River Po' Folk** at $9.95 each. (Make checks payable to **QUIXOTE PRESS.**)

Name _______________________________________

Street _______________________________________

City _________________ State _______ Zip _______

Send Orders To:
Quixote Press
R.R. #4, Box 33B • Blvd. Station
Sioux City, Iowa 51109

(163)

MISSISSIPPI RIVER PO' FOLK
  by Pat Wallace . . . . paperback $9.95

STRANGE FOLKS ALONG THE MISSISSIPPI
  by Pat Wallace . . . . paperback $9.95

THE VANISHING OUTHOUSE OF IOWA
  by Bruce Carlson. . . . . paperback $9.95

THE VANISHING OUTHOUSE OF ILLINOIS
  by Bruce Carlson. . . . . paperback $9.95

THE VANISHING OUTHOUSE OF MINNESOTA
  by Bruce Carlson. . . . . paperback $9.95

THE VANISHING OUTHOUSE OF WISCONSIN
  by Bruce Carlson. . . . . paperback $9.95

MISSISSIPPI RIVER COOKIN' BOOK
  by Bruce Carlson . . . . paperback $11.95

IOWA'S ROAD KILL COOKBOOK
  by Bruce Carlson. . . . . paperback $7.95

HITCH HIKING THE UPPER MIDWEST
  by Bruce Carlson . . . . paperback $7.95

IOWA, THE LAND BETWEEN THE VOWELS
  by Bruce Carlson. . . . . paperback $9.95
        (Farm Boy Stories From the Early 1900's)

GHOSTS OF SOUTHWEST MINNESOTA
  by Ruth Hein . . . . paperback $9.95

GHOSTS OF THE COAST OF MAINE
  by Carole Olivieri Schulte . . . . paperback $9.95

ME 'N WESLEY
  by Bruce Carlson. . . . . paperback $9.95
(Stories about the homemade toys that farm children made and played with around the turn of the century.)

SOUTH DAKOTA ROAD KILL COOKBOOK
by Bruce Carlson . . . . .paperback $7.95

GHOSTS OF THE BLACK HILLS
by Tom Welch. . . . . .paperback $9.95

**Some Pretty Tame, But Kinda Funny Stories
About Early DAKOTA
LADIES-OF-THE-EVENING**
by Tom Welch. . . . . .paperback $9.95

**Some Pretty Tame, But Kinda Funny Stories
About Early IOWA LADIES-OF-THE EVENING**
by Bruce Carlson . . . . paperback $9.95

**Some Pretty Tame, But Kinda Funny Stories
About Early ILLINOIS LADIES-OF-THE-EVENING**
by Bruce Carlson . . . . .paperback $9.95

**Some Pretty Tame, But Kinda Funny Stories
About Early MINNESOTA
LADIES-OF-THE-EVENING**
by Bruce Carlson . . . . .paperback $9.95

**Some Pretty Tame, But Kinda Funny Stories
About Early WISCONSIN
  LADIES-OF-THE-EVENING**
by Bruce Carlson . . . . .paperback $9.95

**Some Pretty Tame, But Kinda Funny Stories
About Early MISSOURI LADIES-OF-THE-EVENING**
by Bruce Carlson . . . . .paperback $9.95

THE DAKOTA'S VANISHING OUTHOUSE
Bruce Carlson . . . . .paperback $9.95

ILLINOIS' ROAD KILL COOKBOOK
by Bruce Carlson . . . . .paperback $7.95

OLD IOWA HOUSES, YOUNG LOVES
by Bruce Carlson . . . . .paperback $9.95
(Stores about old houses in Iowa and young loves they have known.)

TERROR IN THE BLACK HILLS

by Dick Kennedy ....paperback $9.95

IOWA'S EARLY HOME REMEDIES

by 26 students at Wapello Elem. School ...paperback $9.95

INDEX

Chapter titles are shown in capital letters.

INDEX